Router Projects for the Home

Router Projects for the Home

GUILD OF MASTER CRAFTSMAN PUBLICATIONS LTD

This collection first published 1999 by
Guild of Master Craftsman Publications Ltd,
Castle Place, 166 High Street, Lewes,
East Sussex BN7 1XU

© GMC Publications 1999

ISBN   1 86108 112 X

A catalogue record of this book is available from the British Library

Front cover photographs: Anthony Bailey; Front cover illustration: Ian Hall
Back cover photographs: Les Oliver (top), Anthony Bailey (bottom)
Article photography by: Anthony Bailey (pp. 6–9, 87–90, 112–113, 115–116),
Colin Eden-Eadon (p. 35), Alan Goodsell (pp. 40–42)

Other photographs by the authors

Illustrations by Simon Rodway except:
Jack Cox (pp. 54, 55, 56, 57, 58, 80, 81, 82), Ian Hall (pp. 66, 67 and 68),
Trend Routing Technology (p. 86)

Designed by Edward Le Froy and Jenni Keeble

Printed and bound by Kyodo Printing (Singapore) under the supervision of
MRM Graphics, Winslow, Buckinghamshire, UK

Contents

Introduction   1

KITCHEN/DINING ROOM PROJECTS

Salt 'n' pepper   2
Bill Cain makes a **salt and pepper mill** condiment holder

Off your trolley   6
Mark Constanduros cooks up a **kitchen work trolley**
with chopping block

Wholemeal roll   10
Bill Cain devises a **bread box and board** combo

Divide and rule   15
Bill Cain makes a **cutlery tray** for a drawer

Tall story at the bar   20
Betty McKeggie describes the making of a **kitchen stool**
by husband Bill

Drained and bored   24
Colin Eden-Eadon dispels that sinking feeling by making
his own **draining board**

Table for under a ton   26
Les Oliver makes a **circular extending dining table**

Rout of two halves   31
Bob Adsett gets into rural mood to make a **half-glazed
stable door**

Make mine a double   35
Colin Eden-Eadon fits the **half-glazed stable door** made
by Bob Adsett

LIVING ROOM PROJECTS

Burning bright   36
Anthony Bailey makes a **candle sconce with mirror**

In the frame   40
Roger Smith's **picture/mirror frame** requires precision

Stock answer   43
Bill Cain makes an **occasional/coffee table** in limed oak

Knockout archway   48
Lee Ninham tidies up a demolished wall with a **decorative
arch with columns**

Face value   53
Jack Cox makes an attractive **clock face** using his pivot-frame

Armed against argument   59
Bob Curran makes a **height-adjustable two-arm lamp**

Under the thumb   65
Ian Hall makes a small **wall-mounted display cabinet**

Stoke the fire   69
Anthony Bailey warms up his router making a **pine fireplace
surround**

Radiating style   73
Anthony Bailey with some hot tips on making **radiator covers**

BEDROOM PROJECTS

Arcs and parquetry   78
Jack Cox goes full circle engineering a **hand mirror**

Boxercise class   83
Jim Phillips routs a little **trinket box** from the solid

Boxes of tricks   87
Alan Goodsell creates a versatile **bedside cabinet cum
desk cum dressing table**

Bed and boards   Part I   93
Anthony Bailey makes a **headboard and matching
footboard** for a bed

Making Connections   Part II   98
Anthony Bailey adds **frame and slats** to his bed project

Russian under the bed   Part III   103
Anthony Bailey makes a **storage drawer** to go under the bed

Blanket coverage   107
Anthony Bailey makes a beautiful copy of an early **oak
blanket chest**

Mid-winter night's screen   112
Guy Smith makes a versatile **folding screen**

Metric/imperial conversion chart   117

Index   118

Note

Every effort has been made to ensure that the information in this book is accurate at the time of writing but inevitably prices, specifications, and availability of tools will change from time to time. Readers are therefore urged to contact manufacturers or suppliers for up-to-date information before ordering tools.

Measurements

Throughout the book instances may be found where a metric measurement has fractionally varying imperial equivalents, usually within $\frac{1}{16}$in either way. This is because in each particular case the closest imperial equivalent has been given.

A mixture of metric and imperial measurements should NEVER be used – always use either one or the other.

See also detailed metric/imperial conversion charts on page 117.

Introduction

OUR HOMES are dear to all our hearts, unsurprisingly, as they are where we spend most of our free time. It follows, then, that in our quest to make them places to be proud of, they mop up most of our spare cash.

The desirable objects with which we furnish our living spaces are chosen not just for practical purposes but to reflect our individual characters. Bought-in items can be fearsomely expensive, and even those that are affordable will always represent someone else's idea of what is an attractive and functional design.

With this in mind, the best way to own exactly what you want is to make your own items. This may seem a daunting task to many and those who are not woodworkers will doubtless claim that the outlay for equipment excludes delving into this satisfying subject. Not so! A router is the answer. This most useful of tools is inexpensive and, with the addition of a few shop-bought accessories or hand-made jigs, plus a few well-selected cutters, can carry out even the most demanding woodworking tasks.

It is the most versatile of woodworking power tools, enabling the creation of all the attractive and practical projects in this book either just as they are, or modified to suit your own style. The result of your enjoyable hours of making will be a home adorned with all the things you desire.

So take a look around yours, from kitchen through to dining room and sitting room, and finally up to the bedroom, to see how your router could be the tool responsible for achieving the home of your dreams.

Alan Goodsell
Editor, *The Router*

▲ *Finished article with and without pepper mills*

Salt 'n' pepper

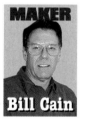

MAKER

Bill Cain

Bill Cain makes a condiment holder

T HE Editor phoned me to say that he was looking for a small and simple, yet challenging, mini-project; it should be an article that was useful, and that looked good. A bit of a tall order – but by pure chance, my daughter then asked me if I could make her a salt and pepper mill holder, similar to one I had made for her mother a while ago – and so I had the opportunity to kill two birds with one stone.

Materials
I decided to use quarter-sawn European oak (*Quercus petraea*) for the sides, ends, and handle, as the grain was right for the thin section and should remain stable, even if washed. It would, of course, look good in almost anything; the 6mm (¼in) section is perhaps a little too thin for softwoods but

you could always run a test piece, or change the section to suit your material.

The size of the holder needs to take into account your own mills; I have worked on internal box sizes of 60 by 60mm (2⅜ by 2 ⅜in) as this takes two 55 by 155mm high (2 by 6in) mills nicely.

Preparation
Construction is quite straightforward but, since it is basically a box, care is called for in preparing the stock thickness, marking out, and finishing to size. I always use a digital vernier calliper for gauging thickness, a steel rule and a stand-mounted magnifying 2x glass for measuring – and a surgeon's old scalpel scribed against an engineer's metal square for most of my marking out!

"I use a surgeon's old scalpel scribed against an engineer's metal square for most of my marking out!"

▼ *Drilling the handle with pillar drill and Forstner bit – note the waste below the work to ensure a clean breakout of the drill bit*

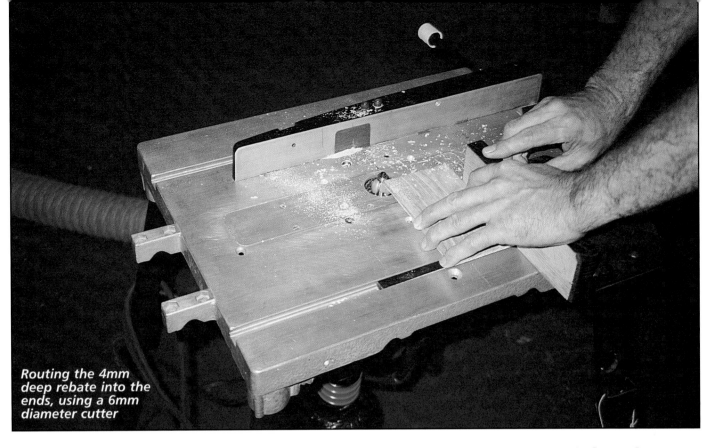

Routing the 4mm deep rebate into the ends, using a 6mm diameter cutter

No difficult joints are called for, but if you fancy a bit more of a challenge, then go ahead and dovetail the corners.

A 6mm (¼in) diameter, depending on the material thickness chosen, 2 flute TCT straight cutter, plus a moulding cutter for the edge of the base, will be required. I chose to use a bearing guided 9.5mm (⅜in) radius TCT cutter with a 12.7mm (¹⁄₁₆in) diameter bearing.

All of my routing was done with an Elu

"No difficult joints are called for, but if you fancy a bit more of a challenge, then go ahead and dovetail the corners by hand"

177E inverted in an Elu table, but if a table is not available, the routing can be

done by hand using a small portable router and its fence, providing extra care is taken.

Routing the middle housing groove across the base – note the waste clamped to the cross-slide to ensure a clean breakout of the cutter

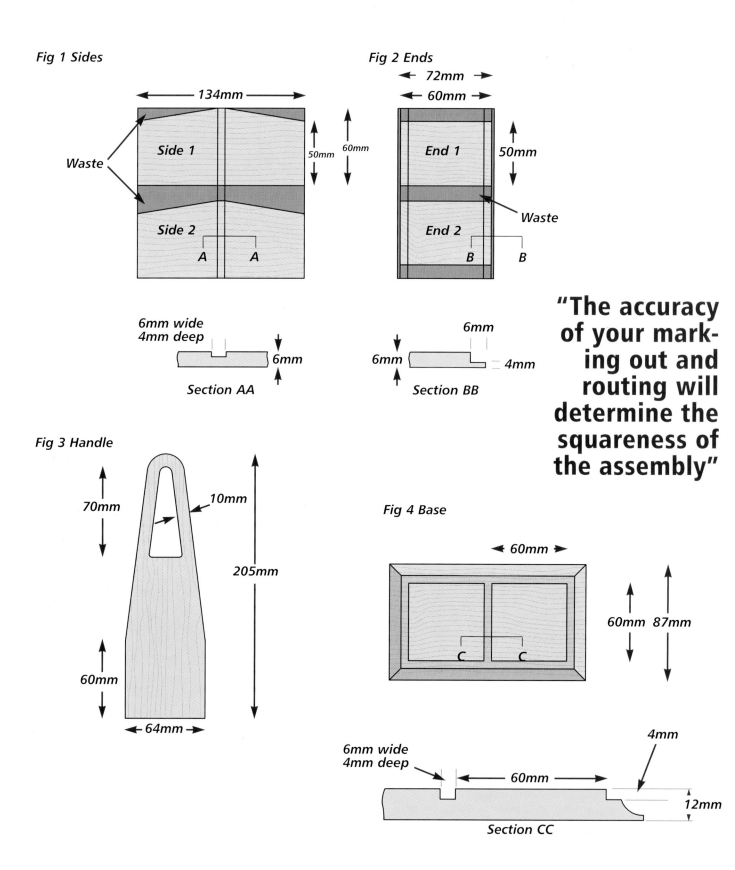

Fig 1 Sides

134mm

Waste

Side 1

Side 2

A   A

50mm   60mm

6mm wide
4mm deep

6mm

Section AA

Fig 2 Ends

72mm

60mm

End 1

End 2

Waste

B   B

50mm

6mm

6mm

6mm

4mm

Section BB

"The accuracy of your marking out and routing will determine the squareness of the assembly"

Fig 3 Handle

70mm

10mm

205mm

60mm

64mm

Fig 4 Base

60mm

60mm 87mm

C   C

6mm wide
4mm deep

60mm

4mm

12mm

Section CC

Construction

Prepare stock by thicknessing to 6mm (¼in), mark out and cut the sides to length, and the ends to width. If you have a table or inverted router then by means of the cross slide, set at 90°, you can trim to size by gauging against the fence. The waste is always useful for setting or trial cuts.

As you will see, the parts are made as pairs and sawn and finished to size after routing. This method provides a longer base for the fence to run on, which is more stable and accurate, and ensures that the various parts are the same size as their opposites. I suggest that you leave the width of the ends oversize, say 1mm (½in), so that they may be finished flush with the sides after gluing, so ensuring crisp corners.

Rout the central groove across the sides and saw and finish the sloped sides as a matched pair.

Mark out the central divider and handle, allowing for whatever depth of groove, times two, you select to rout into the sides when setting out the width.

The shape of the handle is a personal choice; mine was drilled at the top and bottom corners with Forstner bits, in a pillar drill, and then routed out parallel to the finished handle sides using the router table fence and cross slide. A fret saw would produce a similar result.

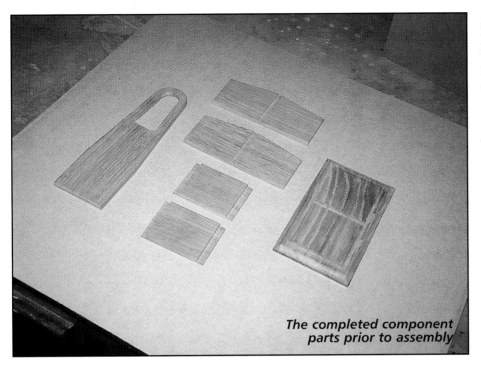

The completed component parts prior to assembly

groove into which the central divider or handle will sit. Finally, rout a moulding of your choice around the edge of the base, but remember not to undercut the rebate or landing for the sides and ends. I went deep enough with the cutter to leave a small, about 1mm (½₂ in), landing around the edge where the sides and base meet.

Assembly and finishing

Dry assemble and check for snug fitting of all parts; if all goes well and you have been accurate, then the parts will assemble nicely, if not, a little 'fitting' may be called for. Sand all parts before gluing.

Glue up and cramp all parts simultaneously with a vice and small lightweight cramps – the accuracy of your marking out and routing will determine the squareness of the assembly. Since this is an article to be used in a kitchen, I would suggest the use of an exterior grade adhesive such as Titebond 2, Evostick Resin W, or Cascamite.

Complete the ends by hand planing the top slope and, with a chisel, carefully pare the width to match the sides.

Finish all over with Danish Oil or similar.

So there you have it, no more loose ground salt or pepper from the mills dropping onto the table top or kitchen work surface! ●

The inset bottom, made from 12mm thick stock, is then marked out and finished to size.

Set the fence to produce the finished internal box sizes, 60 by 60mm (2⅜ by 2⅜in) and rout the edge rebates into which the sides and ends will sit. If you have a larger diameter cutter, or better still, a suitable size rebate cutter, this could be done in a single pass; if not, progressive passes with the 6mm diameter cutter will do the job.

Set up and rout the middle housing

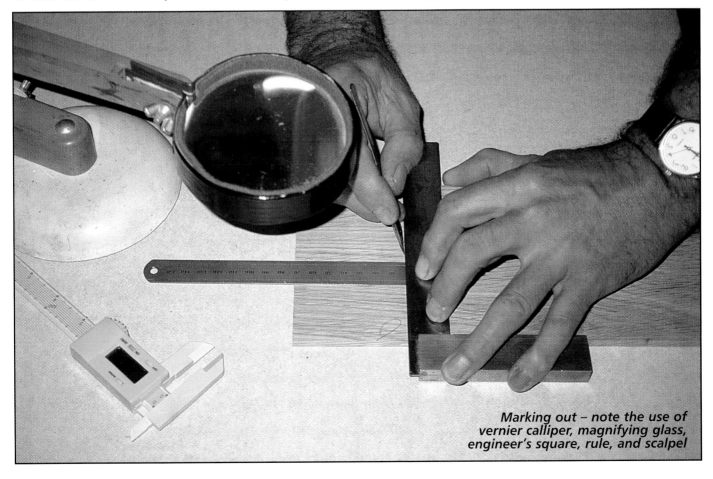

Marking out – note the use of vernier calliper, magnifying glass, engineer's square, rule, and scalpel

Off your trolley

MAKER

Mark Constanduras

Mark Constanduros cooks up a kitchen work trolley with chopping block

N O SOONER had I bought and moved into my small cottage than I realised that my kitchen was rather lacking in the worktop department.

I sat down for a few hours with pencil and paper trying all possibilities to redesign the room so as to create more surface area. Each time my brilliant plans were thwarted by something like a door or window.

In fact I had abandoned the search when, some time later, the solution presented itself to me. Flicking through Dave Mackenzie's book *Pine Furniture Projects For the Home*, I spied his design for a kitchen trolley with a chopping block — just the job!

Ignoring his dimensions and omitting the towel rail and shelf, I set about making one to suit my own kitchen. Its construction is based upon the use of a router.

A visit to the local DIY store produced the timber and hardware components. A sort through the pile of pre-machined pine revealed some straight lengths. Then it was a simple matter of selecting drawer runners, castors and screws.

Frame

Cut four 45 by 45mm (1^3/$_4$ by 1^3/$_4$in) legs to the full 820mm (32^1/$_4$in) height of the trolley then, from the end chosen as the top, mark mortices centrally and the width of the tenon minus haunches.

Cut the mortices with an 8mm diameter straight two-flute cutter and set up the router using an offcut of the timber of the same dimensions. Fasten it securely to the bench with a cramp alongside another piece of wood of the same thickness.

This supports the baseplate of the router and allows a side fence to be used when routing the mortices.

Set the side fence and depth stops to position and carefully rout the mortice in a series of steps so as not to strain the router or cutter. When happy with the result, continue to rout the mortices on all the legs.

Then rout the mortices and housings for the rails above and below the drawer front.

Mark out the tenons and again practise machining on scrap. With an 18mm diameter straight two-flute cutter installed in the router and a side fence fitted, the tenon is machined on either side of the rail.

Set up the depth stop and position the side fence so that the shoulder of the tenon is cut with it running on the end of the tenon. Then use the router free-hand to cut away the waste timber in a number of stages.

When done, cut off the end and haunches — size isn't critical for the tail piece — and place in the mortice to check for a good fit. If it isn't, adjust

▲ *Routing mortices using an extra piece of wood to support the base plate*

"This supports the baseplate of the router and allows a side fence to be used when routing the mortices"

▲ *A piece of wood next to the rail stops the router from dropping when routing their tenons*

▲ *Rout steps on the ends of the drawer rails*

the settings on the router and try again until it is — fine adjusters on the depth stop and side fence are useful for precise settings but they are often an extra.

Mark the rails for their tenons and rout them all, then trim to length and cut their haunches.

Cut the top and bottom drawer rails to length and notch them to fit their housings.

Round off the edges of the legs with a 3.5mm rounding-over cutter, then sand all components thoroughly before gluing and cramping the frame together. A screw through each end of the top drawer rails holds it in place.

When dry, glue and screw the 90 by 90mm triangular corner blocks, through which the chopping block is screwed, flush with the upper edge of the rails.

Slatted shelves

The shelves are the full width of the frame from leg to leg minus 7mm — the size of their rounded edges combined.

Measure the relevant dimensions — necessary for cutting the timber to length — not forgetting to calculate for the housings.

The frame for the shelves is made from 42 by 20mm (1⅝ by ¾in) timber, and is constructed by using a single cut from an 8mm straight two-flute cutter to create a housing.

To hide the joint behind the legs, rout the housings in the shorter rails, cutting about two-thirds of the way through; a piece of timber fixed to the bench will help to support the router while machining.

With the same cutter, rout the

tenons to fit the housings, making sure the face and edges are flush. Sand up the components, then glue and cramp the frames together; measuring the diagonals ensures that they're square.

Cut six 43 by 12mm (1¾in by ½in) slats to length for each shelf then, using the 3.5mm rounding-over cutter, rout the top two edges. Drill and sand the slats before fixing them to the frame with brass screws.

The finished shelves are then screwed to legs from inside.

Drawer

The drawer box is made from 100 by 20mm (4 by ¾in) timber, employing the same bare-faced housing joint as that on the shelf frames. The runners, obtained from the DIY shop, are the bottom-mounted variety which allow the 6mm plywood drawer

bottom to be screwed directly onto the underside of the drawer box through the bottom.

The drawer box width is the measurement between the two front legs minus the thickness of the pair of drawer runners, normally 25mm (1in) — a thin piece of wood on either side of the rails is needed to pack out the runners flush to the legs.

The runners are positioned the thickness of the drawer front, 20mm (¾in), back from the front face of the leg.

The 400mm (15¾in) depth of the drawer box is the same as the length of the runners.

After routing the joints and assembling the drawer box check that it is square across the diagonals. Then make a false drawer front the size of the aperture less about 1.5mm all round, position it centrally, and screw

▲ The top drawer rail is screwed into its housing

▲ The router set up to cut housings in the shelf frame and drawer boxes

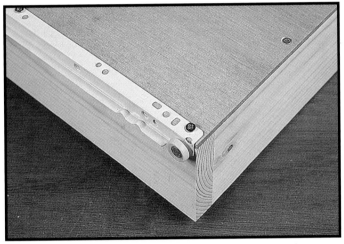

▲ Bottom-mounted drawer runners hold the drawer bottom in place

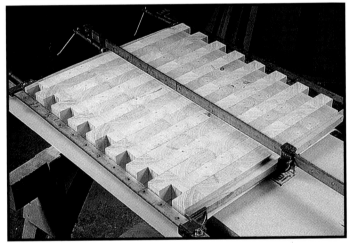

▲ The clamped-up chopping block showing the staggered joint lines

Front and side elevations

725
45
570
170
170
820
780
251
45
12
42
650
500

to the drawer box from inside.

For decoration and before fixing, use the 3.5mm rounding-over cutter. Set it so it cuts a little step and rout it around the edge of the drawer front, starting across the grain to avoid breakout.

The last job is to fit the 38mm (1½in) diameter wooden knob.

Chopping block

Normally a chopping block is made from beech (*Fagus sp*) laid on its end-grain, but to keep costs down pine makes a reasonable alternative.

I used four 850mm (33½in) lengths of planed timber 152 by 50mm (6 by 2in) and one length of 75 by 50mm (3 by 2in).

Lay them side by side and glue them together in board with the narrow piece on one side. When the glue has dried cut 16 slices 45mm (1¾in) long off the end.

▲ *A finished slatted shelf*

▲ *The drawer box features a simple bare-faced housing joint*

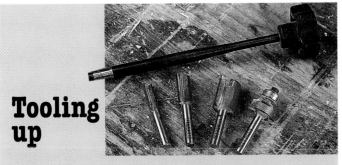

Tooling up

- ■ *8mm diameter straight two-flute cutter*
- ■ *10mm diameter straight two-flute cutter*
- ■ *18mm diameter straight two-flute cutter*
- ■ *3.5mm rounding-over cutter*
- ■ *A fine adjuster is a useful accessory*

"To hide the joint behind the legs, rout the housings in the shorter rails, cutting about two-thirds of the way through"

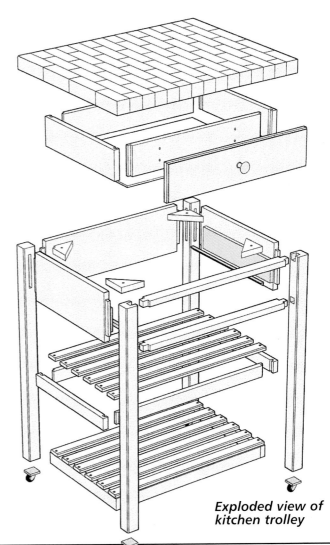

Exploded view of kitchen trolley

With the grain running vertically, place the strips together so that the 75 by 50mm (3 by 2in) pieces are on alternate sides, and stagger the joins by 32mm (1¹/₄in) like brickwork.

With the layout planned mark their positions in relation to each other and move the pieces apart. Spread copious amounts of waterproof glue on the joining faces and place them back together, lining up the marks and cramping them up tightly.

Once the glue is absolutely dry cut the top to size and sand the top thoroughly so it is nice and flat.

The top is screwed to the frame from the underneath through the corner blocks.

Finishing

Castors are available from most DIY stores. Mine are a little small and not lockable. It is possible to get larger, lockable ones but they may have to be ordered and will be more expensive.

When the height of the castors is known the ends of the legs can be trimmed off to accommodate them before they are fitted.

I applied three coats of clear matt polyurethane varnish, chosen for its resistance to water and durability.

Because the chopping block is to be used for food it should be treated with vegetable oil. ●

■ *Pine Furniture Projects for the Home*, by Dave Mackenzie, is available from GMC Publications at £9.95 and can be ordered through Books by Post, 2 Church Lane East, Aldershot, Hants GU11 3BT.

Wholemeal roll

Bill Cain uses his loaf to come up with a roll-top breadbox and board combo

Bill Cain

OUR oak breadboard was a wedding gift 31 years ago, and the pine breadbox of early '80s' vintage – clearly both were past their 'best before' date.

To save valuable worktop space I decided to replace them with a combination of the two, choosing sycamore (*Acer pseudoplatanus*) as this would not taint the bread, is free-cutting and takes on a delightfully creamy, silk-like finish.

As far as size goes, check that the dimensions of your box will fit your daily bread.

I bought my timber as sawn boards from David Simmonds' Interesting Timbers yard near Bath. To ensure stability, select material for the slats and sides that is close

to quarter-sawn.

All routing was achieved with an Elu 177E inverted in an Elu table; the cutters used are as listed, *see Tooling up panel*, but can be varied to suit what you have available.

Box carcass

Prepare stock to 16mm (⅝in) thickness; to ensure that the external shape and pivot points are consistent left-hand to right-hand, profile-rout the sides to a template.

Spot-drill the pivot hole centres from the template and open these out to 8mm diameter by 5mm deep (⁵⁄₁₆ by ¹³⁄₆₄in), using a pillar drill if available.

Rout the 22mm wide by 8mm deep (⅞ by ⁵⁄₁₆in) slot for the breadboard housing,

stopping the cut 12mm (¹⁵⁄₃₂in) short of the back face. Clean out and square off the cut with a chisel, so that the slot aligns with the inside face of the back.

The slot width for the hardboard bottom should be routed, to suit the material thickness by 4mm (⁵⁄₃₂in) deep. I used a ⅛in diameter single-flute HSS cutter, making two passes and adjusting the table fence to obtain the required width.

Stop the cut 8mm (⁵⁄₁₆in) short at both the front and back so as to prevent the slot from being seen after assembly.

Make the back, top and front infill from 12mm (¹⁵⁄₃₂in) prepared stock.

Rout a 1 by 1mm (³⁄₆₄ by ³⁄₆₄in) chamfer on the top faces of the infill strip. If you wish to round-over or otherwise decorate

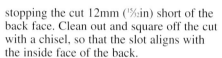

"Sycamore would not taint the bread, is free-cutting and takes on a delightfully creamy, silk-like finish"

▲ *A neat combination of breadbox and cutting board*

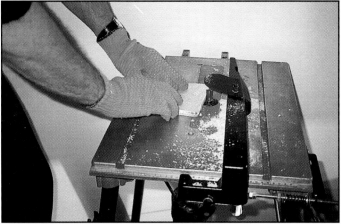

▲ Routing the quadrant profile, using an MDF template plus top-bearing-guided cutter – note the use of guard over the top of the cutter

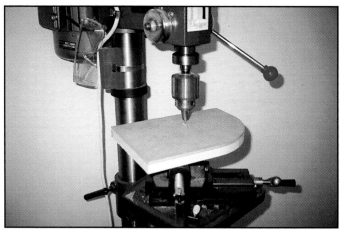

▲ Spotting off the pivot holes in the sides from the template on a pillar drill following routing – use the same procedure for the quadrants

"Using a Trend biscuit-jointing set with the router inverted in the table produces consistent results at less expense than that incurred by investing in a dedicated jointer"

the edge of the top, then this should be done now since you will be unable to get a bearing-guided moulding cutter onto the front face after carcass assembly.

▼ Cutting the biscuit joints into the sides with a table-mounted router and Trend cutter set – note that for safety the work is clamped to an engineering angle plate

Biscuits, dowels

The carcass is biscuit-jointed and dowelled together with size 0 biscuits and 6mm (¼in) dowels, using a Trend biscuit-jointing set with the router inverted in the table, a combination that produces consistent results at less expense than that incurred by investing in a dedicated jointer.

Mark off the biscuit position and, for safety's and squareness of cuts' sake if cutting on an inverted router, clamp the work to an angle plate.

This aid is well worth having for routing and drilling operations, and is easily made from ply or MDF – better still, seek out a second-hand cast-iron or steel example.

Drill the ends of the front infill for the dowels, and drill their mating holes into the sides.

Cut the bottom to size from melamine-faced hardboard.

Assemble all parts dry, and finish sand all interior faces.

Glue-up

This is when the fun starts! With this number of biscuits and faces coming together at the same time, it is essential to establish the clamping method and have everything to hand before gluing – and even then the process could be a bit hectic.

I successfully used Titebond 2, but if I made a second example then I would choose an adhesive with a more generous open time.

Clean up and finish sand the fully assembled carcass.

Roll-top

A little more grey matter has to be employed now. Considering the need or otherwise of a jig to assist in assembling the slats to their quadrants, I concluded that, with care, the box carcass could be used as the assembly medium; but, if making more than a 'one-off', a simple jig would be well worth the effort of devising, speeding up and easing the operation.

"An angle plate is well worth having for routing and drilling operations, and is easily made from ply or MDF – better still, seek out a second-hand cast-iron or steel example"

Tooling up

- Trend TCT bearing-guided biscuit jointer set
- Titman TCT top-bearing-guided 16mm diameter profile cutter
- Titman TCT straight two-flute 18.5mm (¾in) diameter cutter
- Titman TCT bearing-guided 9.5mm radius rounding-over cutter
- Sears Craftsman (USA) TCT bull-nose 12.7mm (½in) diameter gutter cutter
- Sears Craftsman (USA) HSS single-flute 3mm (⅛in) cutter

▲Cutters used

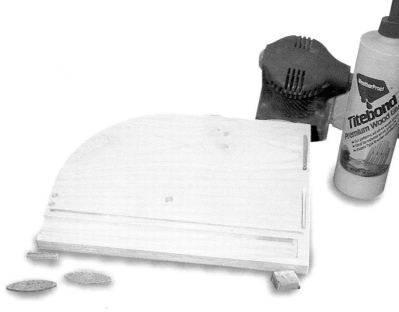

The geometry of the quadrants requires careful marking out and routing since they must be identical.

Using the template, profile-rout all the external faces of the quadrants and, with the template still in position, and using a pillar drill if available, drill off the 8mm (⁵⁄₁₆in) diameter pivot holes.

Make and glue to the outside faces of each quadrant a 1mm-thick (³⁄₆₄in) 'washer' to the pivot area. I used birch multi-ply reduced on the bandsaw to the required thickness – about two laminations. On assembly, this controls the necessary 1mm clearance between the quadrant and the box carcass.

Prepare sufficient board for the 10 slats – plus a bit more just in case – and thickness to 6mm (¼in). Finish to length.

Rout the 6mm wide by 3mm deep (¼ by ⅛in) rebates at each end and slice off the strips to finish at 23mm (²⁹⁄₃₂in) width.

Rout a 1 by 1mm (³⁄₆₄ by ³⁄₆₄in) chamfer down the length of all interior and exterior faces.

Finish sand all parts.

Roll-top assembly

Because you will have to pull them out later when access is limited, use a couple of long 8mm (⁵⁄₁₆in) diameter dowels to assemble the quadrants to the carcass.

▼ *Routing the front edge of the breadboard, feeding 'downhill' to prevent tearout*

▲ *Sides complete and ready for assembly*

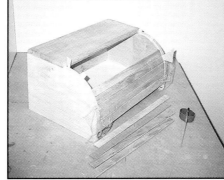

▲ *Gluing slats to quadrants – note use of wedges to hold slats in position, and cling-film to prevent the top from sticking to the sides and bottom rail*

Cut some small, thin wedges and use them to wedge the quadrants into their closed position.

Working upwards from the top face of the carcass infill strip, glue and pin the first six slats to the quadrants.

Place kitchen cling-film between relevant faces to prevent the roll-top from becoming glued to the carcass.

Allow the glue to cure.

Remove the partial assembly from the carcass and glue and pin slats seven to 10 into position.

Open up the pivot holes to an 8mm diameter clearance – say 8.5mm (¹¹⁄₃₂in) diameter – to allow the quadrants to swing freely on an 8mm diameter pivot pin.

Punch the pins below the surface of the slats and fill with a suitable matching filler.

▲ *End view of assembled roll-top, handle and turned pivot pins; the 1mm ply spacer is glued to the pivot area of the quadrant's outside face*

Breadboard

To ensure stability and minimise cupping, the breadboard is constructed from three 20mm-thick (²⁵⁄₃₂in) boards, biscuited together, using the router to cut the biscuit slots; alternatively, a loose ply tongue in stopped slots, or dowels, could be used.

The final shape of the board can be profile-routed to a template. It must, however, project from the carcass when stowed, and I chose to drill a couple of ⅞in diameter finger-pull holes, using a Forstner bit in the pillar drill.

Whatever shape you select, cut 'downhill' with the grain when profile routing as this will assist in preventing end-grain tearout. To achieve this, you will probably have to move the template to the reverse face of the work at some point.

Finally, rout a small chamfer to all edges, and finish sand.

Cutting list

- ■ *1off*   *Breadboard*   *20 by 258 by 398mm (¹³⁄₁₆ by 10³⁄₁₆ by 15¹¹⁄₁₆in)*
- ■ *1off*   *Floor*   *3.5 by 254 by 392mm (⅛ by 10 by 15⁷⁄₁₆in)*
- ■ *10off*   *Slats*   *6 by 23 by 382mm (¼ by ⅞ by 15¹⁄₁₆in)*
- ■ *2off*   *Handles*   *make to suit*
- ■ *2off*   *Quadrants*   *6mm (¼in) thick MDF or ply*

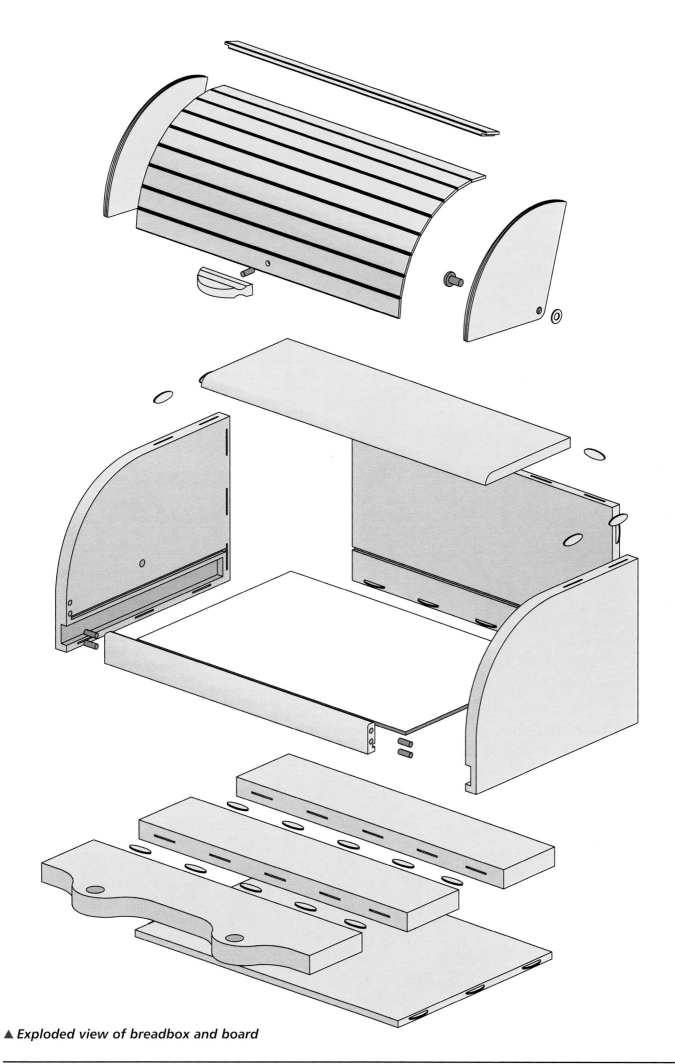

▲ *Exploded view of breadbox and board*

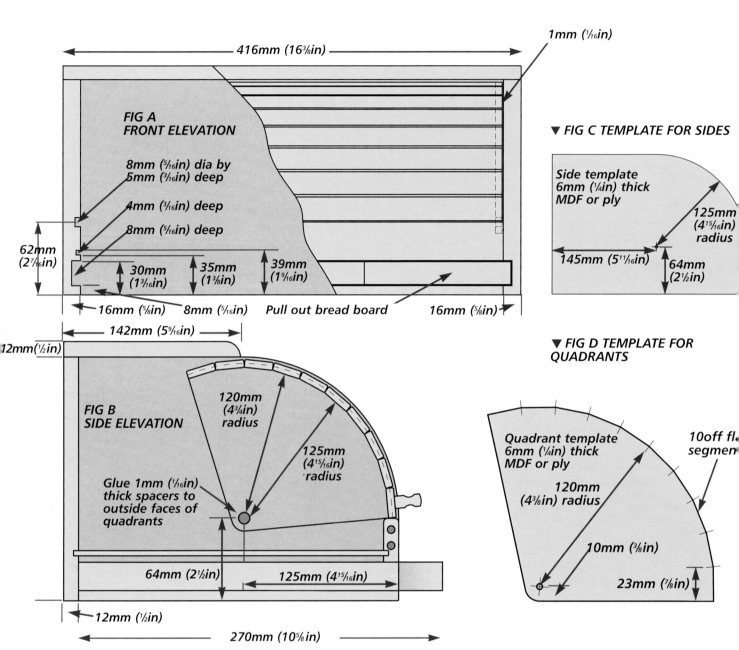

FIG A FRONT ELEVATION

416mm (16³⁄₈in)

1mm (¹⁄₁₆in)

8mm (⁵⁄₁₆in) dia by 5mm (³⁄₁₆in) deep

4mm (³⁄₁₆in) deep

8mm (⁵⁄₁₆in) deep

62mm (2⁷⁄₁₆in)

30mm (1³⁄₁₆in)

35mm (1³⁄₈in)

39mm (1⁹⁄₁₆in)

16mm (⁵⁄₈in)

8mm (⁵⁄₁₆in)

Pull out bread board

16mm (⁵⁄₈in)

▼ FIG C TEMPLATE FOR SIDES

Side template 6mm (¹⁄₄in) thick MDF or ply

125mm (4¹⁵⁄₁₆in) radius

145mm (5¹¹⁄₁₆in)

64mm (2¹⁄₂in)

FIG B SIDE ELEVATION

142mm (5⁹⁄₁₆in)

12mm (¹⁄₂in)

120mm (4³⁄₄in) radius

125mm (4¹⁵⁄₁₆in) radius

Glue 1mm (¹⁄₁₆in) thick spacers to outside faces of quadrants

64mm (2¹⁄₂in)

125mm (4¹⁵⁄₁₆in)

12mm (¹⁄₂in)

270mm (10⁵⁄₈in)

▼ FIG D TEMPLATE FOR QUADRANTS

Quadrant template 6mm (¹⁄₄in) thick MDF or ply

120mm (4³⁄₈in) radius

10mm (³⁄₈in)

10off fl. segmen

23mm (⁷⁄₈in)

Carcass to roll-top

Short, say 16mm (⁵⁄₈in) long, 8mm (⁵⁄₁₆in) diameter, dowelling can be used for the pivot pins. I turned up some button-headed pins for this purpose and for securing the handle to the bottom slat.

I made the pins and handle from sycamore, and the handle incorporates a finger détente routed into top and bottom faces, using a ½in diameter bull-nose gutter cutter.

The final shape is bandsawn and sanded.

Glue and dowel the handle to the bottom slat's front face, position the roll-top assembly into the carcass and push-fit the pivot pins into the sides.

Finishing

Both the box and the board can be left in their natural state, but I chose to seal the box exterior with a couple of coats of Chestnut Finishing Oil, leaving the inside in its taint-free state.

For the sake of initial appearance – no doubt it will wash off – I gave my board a light coat of olive oil. ●

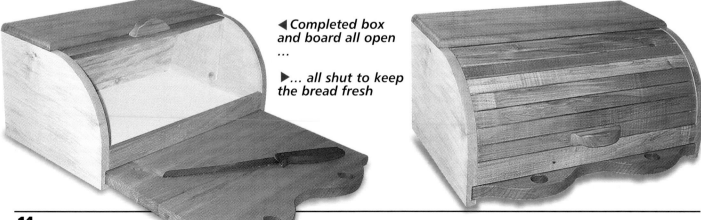

◀ Completed box and board all open ...

▶ ... all shut to keep the bread fresh

Divide
and rule

Bill Cain uses his router to make a cutlery tray for a drawer

A S with my salt and pepper mill holder, *see page 2*, accuracy and care is required at all stages, particularly while preparing the stock, marking out and routing the rebates for this project.

The simplistic basic design should, with care, result in a crisp and functional product.

I lined the interior with traditional green baize, *see panel*, but this can be omitted if you wish.

The sizes must accord with your own internal drawer dimensions, these seeming to vary a great deal despite the fact that most kitchen and dining-room furniture now comes in common external-sized modules.

When adjusting the dimensions to suit your application, take time out to consider how best to minimise the number of router fence and height set-ups. This will reduce the potential for small inaccuracies creeping into the work, in particular in the spacing of grooves for internal dividers.

I would also recommend that all the 2mm (⁵⁄₆₄in) rebates are cut while the router is set to the height setting.

Keep all offcuts of dimensioned stock since these are invaluable for establishing cut height and fence positions when setting up.

I always check these with a digital read-out vernier calliper. This tool has got

▲ *A tray to keep cutlery tidy in the kitchen or dresser drawers*

to be my best buy in a long time, reading a conventional vernier now being beyond my eyesight – put one on the Christmas list right now!

For routing I used an ELU 117E inverted in an ELU table. You could rout freehand, but I suspect that greater care would be required since the material section is relatively small and thin.

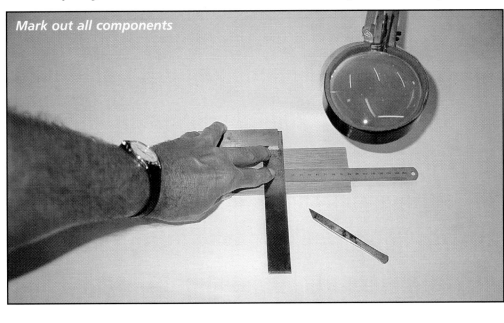

Mark out all components

"This tool has got to be my best buy in a long time, reading a conventional vernier now being beyond my eyesight"

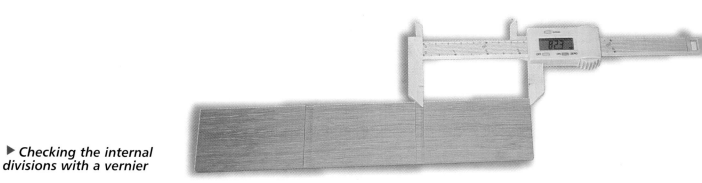

▶ *Checking the internal divisions with a vernier*

"My choice for the frame was European oak since there were plenty of offcuts in the 'come in handy one day' bin"

◀*Rout the housings for the dividers*

▼ *Then machine the housings for the bottom while the cutter is set to the correct depth*

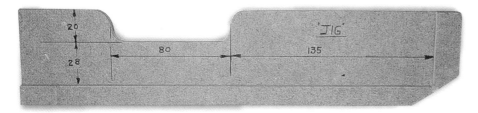

▲ The jig for routing the finger cut-outs

▼ Bandsawing off the excess wood for the finger cut-outs

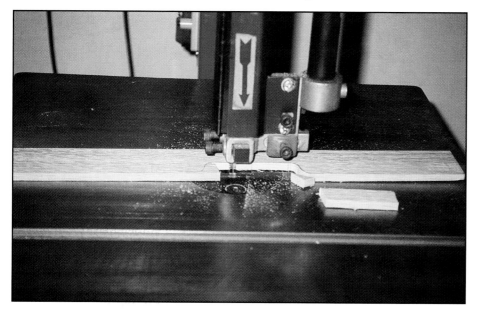

Material, cutters

My choice for the frame was European oak (*Quercus robur*), since there were plenty of offcuts in the 'come in handy one day' bin, but whatever you choose, try to ensure it is relatively straight-grained and, if possible, quarter-sawn.

If you go for softwood then you may need to increase the thickness to 8 or 10mm (⁵⁄₁₆ to ⅜in); run a test piece and see how you feel about it.

The bottom is from 6.3mm (¼in) MDF; birch ply would also be suitable, but I would avoid solid timber due to its natural movement.

I have used only a few cutters, *see*

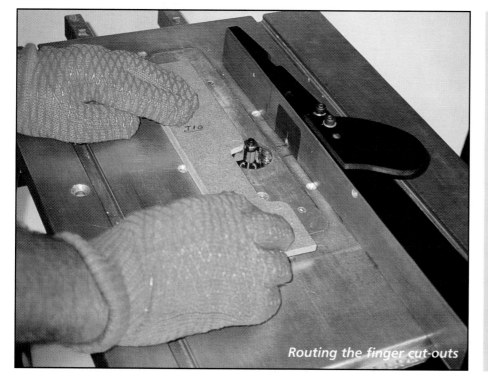

Routing the finger cut-outs

"Prepare sufficient stock to the finished thickness and width – I run an extra length in case of a cock-up"

Tooling Up panel, but unless you feel inclined to add to your stock of cutters your method of construction will depend on what's in your cutter box.

Construction

Prepare sufficient stock to the finished thickness and width – I run an extra length in case of a cock-up – mark out and cut all lengths to the required dimensions. Ensure that the stock is of constant section, with identical lengths, as appropriate, and the ends square at 90°.

Prepare the lengths to be rebated plus 1mm (³⁄₆₄in) oversize to allow for clean-up following assembly, so ensuring crisp corners on the cutlery tray.

Mark out the tray components then set the fences and, with the 6.3mm diameter straight cutter set to a cut depth of 2mm, rout all grooves across the full section, 48mm of the interior dividers.

Groove the ends and side, but stop the cut 12mm (½in) short of the full 60mm (2⅜in) width.

Without moving the cutter height, reset the fence and rout the rebates to the ends of the front and back pieces. Remember to add 0.5mm to the fence setting (1mm overall to allow for the corner clean-up).

Applying baize

The baize may be applied when the finish coating is dry. This material is difficult to cut accurately to size since it can all too easily pull or stretch, and I recommend that paper masking tape be applied to one side, being removed only after cutting to size.

The tape will remove a small amount of the pile as it is taken off, but this should not be a problem with gentle treatment. I find it best to cut the baize 1mm undersize with a new blade in a Stanley knife.

Using Titebond, I smoothed the baize down lightly with a small block of MDF. A light touch with the adhesive and the smoothing is needed to prevent the glue from bleeding through to the top surface of the baize.

▲The components ready to assemble   ▲ The cutlery tray assembled prior to applying the finishing touches

It's when establishing and measuring this sort of setting for cuts that the digital calliper is of great help, see above.

Finally, again without moving the cutter height, reset the fence end cut the full-length grooves for the MDF bottom to sit in.

Dividers

I have profiled three of the interior dividers to provide finger access. A simple 6mm (¼in) thick MDF jig/template ensures that all three cut-outs are in the same relative position and of an identical profile.

So that no time is wasted, I normally glue aids of this sort together with Superglue.

With the work in the jig, draw around the cut-out and, with a bandsaw, jigsaw or coping/fretsaw, remove the bulk of the waste, leaving about 1mm for profiling with the bearing-guided cutter.

I prefer to use a top-bearing cutter because this enables the material being

cut to be observed, the template being below the work on the table face. For greater safety, however, a bottom-bearing cutter is better since the cutter is not so exposed.

Either way, it goes without saying that the cutter should be guarded as best as possible, a suitable glove worn and fingers kept well clear at all times!

If you intend using a bottom-bearing cutter then the jig should be made 'opposite hand' from that shown. This ensures that the cutter thrust pushes the work into the jig.

If you have a variable speed router, keep the spindle speed down and the work always moving during profiling to prevent cutter burn.

For oak, I set my ELU 117E to No. 3, about 16000rpm. If you do end up with a burn, clean it out by running the work back through the cutter in the opposite direction to the cut.

Finish-sand these three dividers then, with a 90° bearing-guided chamfer cutter, apply a 1.5 by 1.5mm (¹⁄₁₆ by ¹⁄₁₆in) chamfer to the cut-outs only. Do not go the full length of the divider, just past the rounded edge will do for now since all the other chamfers will be applied after final assembly.

Leave the chamfer cutter in the router and retain its setting. Finish-sand all remaining parts. Mark out and cut the bottom from 6.3mm (¼in) MDF, being as accurate as possible since the bottom is intended to fit snugly and assist in controlling size and squareness on final assembly.

Assembly

Dry-assemble all parts and establish the method of clamping. Glue up in a single operation, using Titebond or regular PVA.

The bottom, which is glued all around its periphery to induce stiffness to the product,

"It goes without saying that the cutter should be guarded as best as possible, a suitable glove worn and fingers kept well clear at all times"

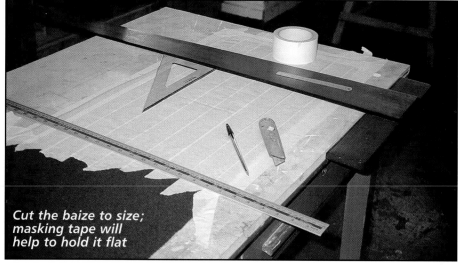

Cut the baize to size; masking tape will help to hold it flat

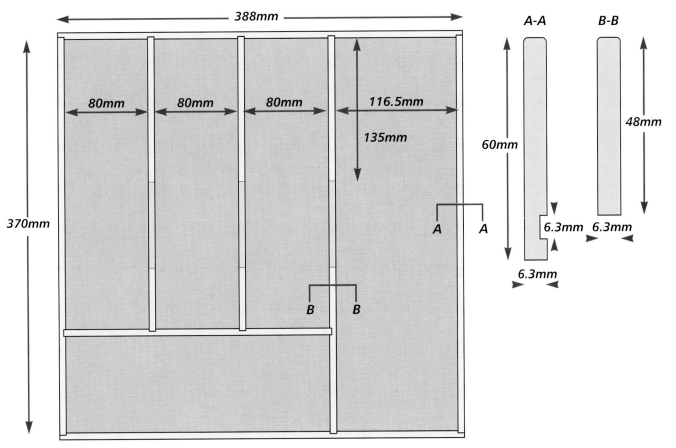

Front

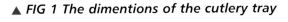

▲ FIG 1 The dimentions of the cutlery tray

▼ FIG 2 Dimensions of jig for finger cut-outs

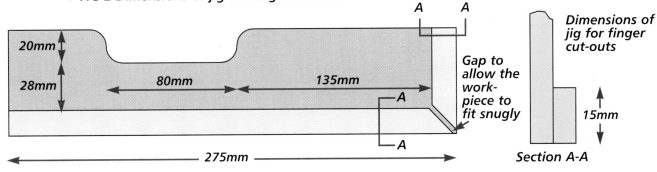

20mm

28mm

80mm

135mm

275mm

A A

Gap to allow the work-piece to fit snugly

Dimensions of jig for finger cut-outs

15mm

Section A-A

should ensure that the finished article is both to size and square, but check it on gluing just in case.

A couple of moulding pins can be added to the corner joints. These should be punched below the surface and filled with a suitable filler.

Clean up and, using the 90° cutter on the same setting, complete the routing of all chamfers. A 90° cutter is essential since this can now only be applied to the top faces. Only a 90° cutter will blend correctly with the previously routed finger cut-out chamfers.

Finishing

I put on two coats of Rustin's Danish Oil, brushing it on and ragging it off to leave thin applications, followed, when dry, with a final wax polishing. Take care not to contaminate the bottom interior if baize is to be applied, *see panel*. ●

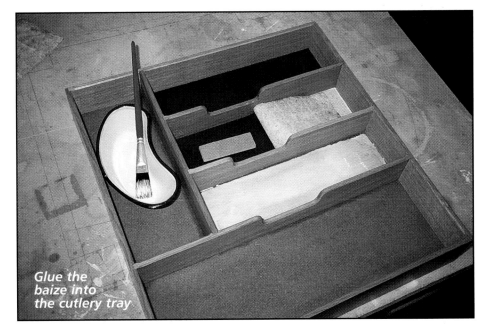

Glue the baize into the cutlery tray

Tall story at the bar

MAKERS

Bill and Betty McKeggie

Betty McKeggie describes the making of a kitchen stool by husband Bill

THE stool described is one of a set of four made for use at a breakfast bar. As workshop and kitchen were 400 miles apart, however, one stool was made first to try out the dimensions.

This one, at 700mm (27½in), proved fine for a child, but adults could not get their legs under the overhang of the bar, so the rest of the set were made 650mm (25½in) high, which proved exactly right.

Apart from use with a breakfast – or any other sort of – bar, a tall stool is useful in any kitchen when time-consuming, tedious jobs make it convenient to sit up to the cooker or bench; taking the weight off your feet makes the job less tiring, *see pic 1.*

Design

This set of stools was made of ash (*Fraxinus sp*), a pleasant, pale wood, straight-grained and strong enough to cope with the stresses and strains to which it would be subjected.

The stools have stood up well to family use, coping with one 17-stone member, a hefty child and his friends.

The finished height was dictated in this case by that of the breakfast bar against which the stools would be used, but if you are making one just for general kitchen use, some thought

"This one proved fine for a child but adults could not get their legs under the overhang of the bar"

▲ *Pic 1 A tall stool is useful in any kitchen or bar*

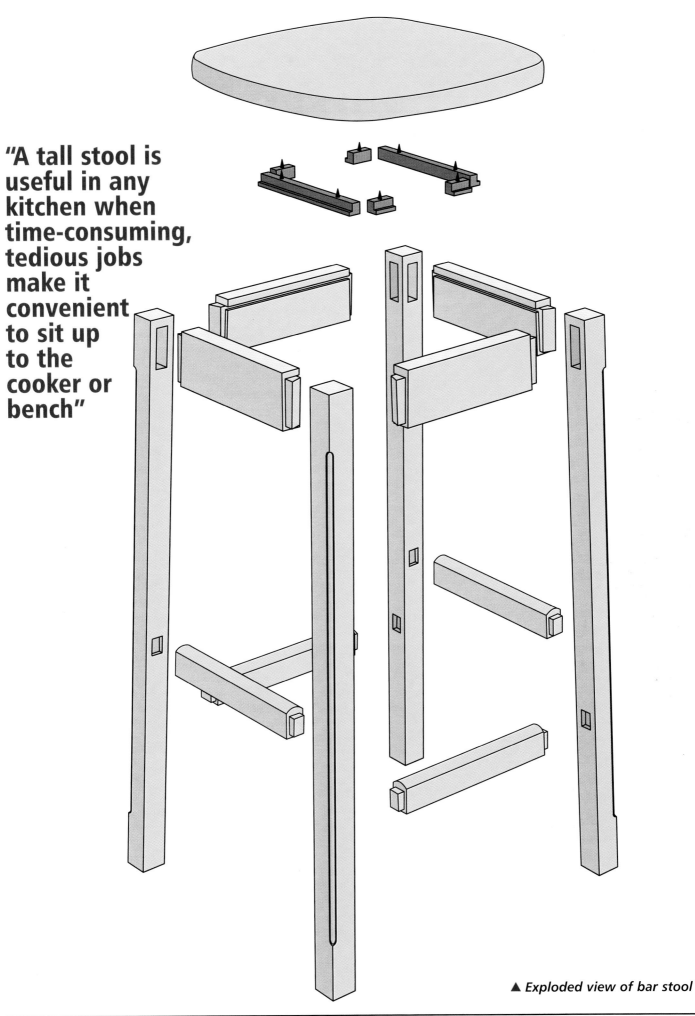

"A tall stool is useful in any kitchen when time-consuming, tedious jobs make it convenient to sit up to the cooker or bench"

▲ *Exploded view of bar stool*

Delivery

Delivering the finished article can present problems to the productive woodworker, if the final destination is some way away.

We found that the cost of sending the set of stools by furniture removers or similar carriers would have been astronomical, even if they went as a part load at the carrier's convenience. Prices around £80 to £100 were quoted.

The problem was solved by removing the seats and making one parcel of them, then putting the stools, minus the seats, inside one another, to form a second.

The two parcels were sent by parcel post, with suitable protective packaging. The overall dimensions came within allowable limits and, because ash is a relatively light wood, the weight was acceptable too. They arrived within a few days quite safely.

▲ *Pic 4 Stool frame, showing angled cramping blocks*

▲ *Pic 2 Detail of ovolo moulding*

▼ *Pic 3 Legs assembled in pairs, with tenoned rails*

should be given to the height relative to that of the people who will use them most.

Children do not seem to mind having to climb up, using the rails as a ladder, but very short or very tall adults might welcome some adjustment of the dimensions. Alternatively, if you just need a stool or stools for a dining-height table, the length of the legs can be reduced, and the position of the rails adjusted to suit.

The legs are splayed out for stability, and their outer edges are moulded for most of their length.

The upper edges of the lower rails are chamfered, and for comfort the seat has rounded corners and edges.

Templates

First, make a full-scale drawing on white-faced hardboard, accurately drawing the angle of the legs' splay. This is so that the rails can be laid on the template to mark out the tenons and their shoulder angles.

To ensure that all the stools in the set match, make a template for the seat so a router can be used to make identical ones. The shape of half the seat is drawn out on a piece of plywood thick enough to accommodate the collar of the guidebush to

be used with the router. Half the seat is formed first, then the template is turned around to form the other half.

If only a single stool is required, the shape may be drawn out directly onto the seat blank and formed to shape by hand.

Construction

Cut the leg pieces to length, allowing a little for final trimming and levelling. The positions of the mortices are marked on the legs in pairs; using a router with a straight cutter fitted, cut them to the correct width, length and depth.

The rails are cut overlong then laid on the hardboard template to mark accurately the lengths of the tenons and the angles and their shoulders. A jig can be made, with an angle built in, so that the tenons can all be accurately and repeatedly cut with a router. Their ends will need trimming with a mitre so that when two tenons enter the same leg they do not interfere with each other.

The rails forming the top frame and support for the seat have a groove cut along their length to accommodate the buttons, or rebated blocks, which secure the seat to the stool. So that the seat will sit flat on the stool the top edge of the rails and the ends of the legs will need planing flat to compensate for the splaying of the legs; a hand plane does the job well.

The outer edge of each leg is moulded using an ovolo router cutter, this moulding stopping approximately 70mm (2¾in) short of the top and bottom, *see pic 2*.

▼ *Pic 5 Seat blank cut to size on a bandsaw; the template is clamped on*

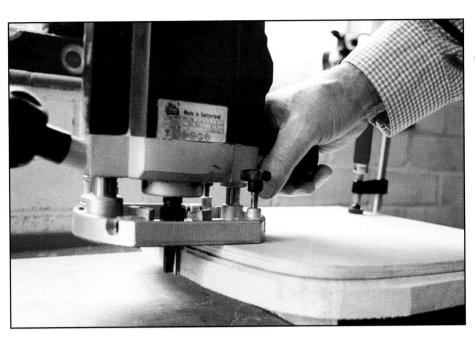

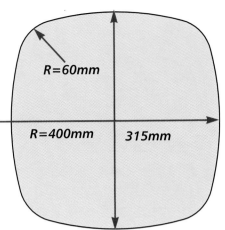

R=60mm

R=400mm   315mm

▲ Underside of seat prior to finishing, with buttons in position

Assembly

Make four blocks of scrap wood with one edge cut to reproduce the angle of the legs, to use as clamping blocks. Then assemble the legs two pairs at a time, laying the assembly on the full-scale drawing to check the angles. They are then glued and clamped, using the angled blocks between the clamps and frame, see pic 3.

When the glue is dry, the two pairs are joined with the remaining rails, again checking the angles on the full-scale drawing, see pic 4.

The rails forming the top, seat-supporting, frame are checked to ensure that they form a square. Measuring across the diagonals will give an accurate reading, and adjustments can be made by placing another clamp across the long diagonal and tightening until square.

▲ *Pic 6 The seat being trimmed, using the template*

Seat

The seat is rough cut slightly oversize, using a bandsaw or jigsaw, see pic 5. Then, using the ply template and a straight router bit with a guidebush fitted into the router's baseplate, the seat is routed to a smooth and uniform finish, see pic 6. The edges are rounded using the router freehand and fitted with a bearing-guided roundover bit.

Two lengths of wood are routed with a rebate and made so they fit into the grooves cut in the top frame rails. Cut off four short pieces, leaving two longer ones.

Traditionally called buttons, these are then positioned into the rail grooves, after finishing, and screwed into the bottom of the seat, see pic 7. This simple way of fixing the seat allows for any expansion or contraction of the timber.

Finishing

After cutting the bottom ends of the legs at a complementary angle to their splay, check that the legs are all level.

Rub down the stool, using successive grades of abrasive paper and, when satisfied that a smooth finish has been achieved, apply two coats of polyurethane varnish, de-nibbing in between coats. ●

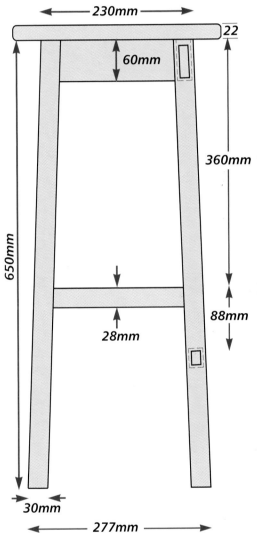

230mm

22

60mm

360mm

650mm

88mm

28mm

30mm

277mm

▲ *Dimensions of bar stool*

Cutting list for one stool

No.	Component	Length	Width	Thickness
4off	Legs	650	30	30
4off	Top rails	220	60	22
2off	Inter. Rails	250	28	22
2off	Bottom rails	258	28	22
1off	Seat	315	315	22

All sizes in millimetres

Tooling up

■ *Trend straight cutter*
■ *Trend ovolo cutter*
■ *Roundover cutter*

▲ A draining board fit for a router project

Drained and bored

MAKER
Colin Eden Eadon

Colin Eden-Eadon dispels that sinking feeling by making his own draining board

H AVING had a butler sink fitted, I needed a draining board pretty swiftly – but a brief and depressing look at the prices for a bought one had me breaking out the router.

Draining boards are traditionally made from maple, but as beech and sycamore are also suitable for kitchen use I opted for easily obtainable sycamore.

The board consists of a main draining centre piece with six tapered grooves, a shallow cutlery well and a simple screwed and plugged frame.

Preparing blank

Plane the wood to size, the main board being 30mm (1³⁄₁₆in) thick and made up to width with two pieces of wood. Overall sizes are 350mm (13¾in) by 585mm (23in).

Ensure their meeting faces are flat and true, ready for biscuit-jointing with the

router. Place the boards joint sides together and mark the biscuit positions across both, using four or five biscuits.

So as not to expose the biscuits, allow enough distance from the ends of the boards for trimming off. Glue and cramp the pieces together, and when dry cut the glued up board to size and clamp it to the bench. To allow water to run off, rout a curve on the front end of the board with a bearing-guided roundover cutter.

Cutlery well

The well is the same 6mm (¼in) depth as the start of the grooves; remember that the grooves deepen at the other end, and that if they are started too deep it may not be possible to achieve the final depth with the short core box cutter; note, too, that if the well is too deep the biscuits may be exposed.

▲ Counterbore and plug cutters make a neat job of screwed joints

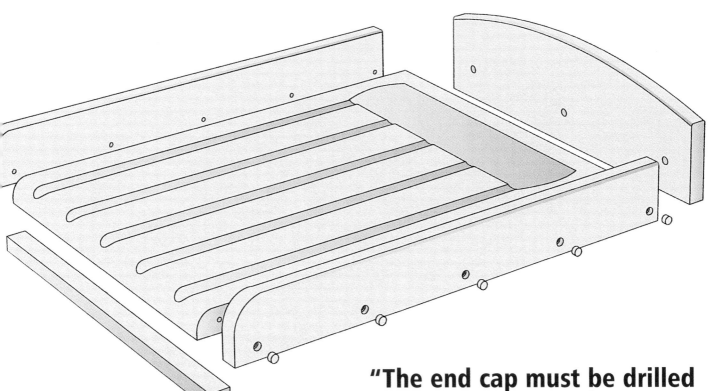

▲ Exploded view of draining board

With a 13mm diameter straight cutter used with a side fence, rout the long cross-grain edges first, and then rout in steps to clean out the bottom. Clean up the ends of the well by routing the short sides.

Produce a rounded edge with the core box cutter.

Cutting grooves

The tapered grooves for the main board are created with a core box cutter and a jig, *see diagram*, made from 6mm ply or MDF. Ply is less likely to bend under the weight of the router, but to be on the safe side fit a small fillet underneath the jig.

Cut a slot in the ply to fit a 17mm diameter guide bush. Allowing for the difference between the cutter and guide bush diameters, carefully mark out the groove positions. Practise on scrap wood first.

▼ Jig for routing grooves

"The end cap must be drilled with a double counterbore, one on each side to allow for movement"

Frame

The side pieces are 22 by 55mm (⅞ by 2⅛in), cut to the same length as the board. The end cap is 100mm (4in) wide and the same thickness.

As a router cannot be plunged at angles other than 90°, it is a natural drilling machine. Cutters are available for drilling and counterboring in one; plug cutters are matched to suit. Adjust the side fence to position the holes.

Cut the curved corners on the side pieces with a bandsaw and clean up. A roundover cutter achieves the rounded edges of the side pieces.

End cap

Cut the curved end cap to length – the board width plus the thickness of the two sides – and make a template from MDF or ply.

Bend a steel rule to mark out the curve, then cut on a bandsaw and clean up. With the template, mark out the curve on the end cap and cut it out a couple of millimetres oversize, then screw it to the template.

Using a template profiling cutter on a table, clean up the curve. Make sure a holding device for the workpiece is attached to the template, and for added safety use a feed on/off pin.

Round the edges with the bearing-guided cutter. The end cap must be drilled with a double counterbore, one on each side to allow for movement.

If you need to raise the board above the lip of a sink you can attach a double counterbored foot to the underside of the front, which will also help with movement.

Sand everything and apply at least five coats of Danish oil to all surfaces, fine sanding between each coat. Screw the assembly together. Glue in the plugs and cut off the excess. Sand flush and apply a finish. ●

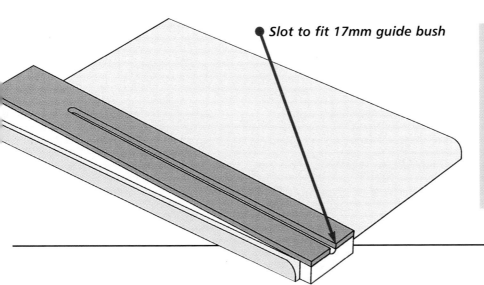

● Slot to fit 17mm guide bush

Tooling up

- Trend biscuit jointer set
- Trend drill and counterbore 9.5mm diameter
- Trend plug maker 9.5mm diameter
- Wealden roundover/ ovolo cutter with bearing
- Wealden core box bit
- Wealden double-flute straight cutter

Table for un

Les Oliver makes a circular extending dining table from an old suspended ceiling

I've always liked circular dining tables which somehow seem to provide more space than rectangular ones of similar dimensions, and the acquisition of a substantial quantity of second-hand mahogany at the right price — free — triggered me into action.

The mahogany had been used as part of a planked design of suspended ceiling, with black Formica-faced tongues in between each grooved and chamfered joint. After removal of the grooves and chamfers I was left with a 45 by 25mm section in average lengths of 2m. I removed the old varnish with Nitromors.

Making top
Because I was after a perfectly flat top with a pleasing grain pattern rather than a planked effect, I dismissed the idea of jointing the planks together. Clearly, the only way to achieve my aim was to go for veneer on a man-made board such as MDF or chipboard.

I chose the latter on the basis that it's cheaper and I have had plenty of experience using it. Also, chipboard appears to stay flatter than MDF.

Start by cutting a 1200mm-square piece of 19mm thick chipboard into a 12-sided shape, then edging it with the mahogany prior to veneering.

Had the mahogany been wider than 45mm, I could have reduced the number of sides, but this would, of course, have produced more end-grain when the circle was cut. I used a saw cutter in my Bosch router to cut a 10mm-deep groove in both the chipboard top and the edging.

The corners were hand-mitred and the edgings then fitted to the top with plywood tongues stuck with Evostik Resin W and cramped in opposite pairs. I allowed about 1mm on the face for cleaning off, leaving a 5mm overhang on the underside.

Halving table
After planing the edgings flush with the chipboard and levelling the joints on the underside, the router comes into play again.

Chipboard 19mm thick provides a stable flat surface. Cut a 1200mm-square piece into a 12-sided shape

Cut a 10mm deep groove in both the chipboard and the mahogany edging prior to gluing and cramping

I drilled a 6mm hole in the centre of the top and fitted a wooden dowel as a pivot. I then made a trammel using extension rods and a plywood cramp so that I could set the router to a radius of 600mm.

I achieved a perfect circle with a straight cutter, setting the depth stop to about 5mm. Taking no more than a 5mm cut each time, the 12-sided shape is quickly converted into a circle. Since the table extends, the circular top must be cut in half and edgings fitted as before.

To ensure a positive location of the two halves during use, a tongue-and-groove joint is created with the router. Locating dowels could also have been used.

Extension piece
Construction of the 600mm-wide centre folding extension piece follows the edging technique. The hinging and fixing of this is covered below.

The round table top needs splitting and edging to allow the top to be extended. For location, either tongue-and-groove or dowel the two halves

The cherry veneering was accomplished by a shopfitting firm, and my final job was to complete the top by forming a moulding around the perimeter. I used an ogee cutter in my router working off the face, and a ovolo cutter from underneath.

Subframe
The subframe provides the means by which the top is joined to the pedestal leg; it gives the folding extension a fixing location and a place to park when not in use; and it provides runners for the two halves of the top to slide on when the extension is in use.

Construction starts with the circular support frame which is built up from 12 segments 25mm thick, cut to the correct radius, butt jointed/glued together. Another course of segments with staggered joints is glued on top.

Only the outer face is radiused, the inner edges being left straight to provide more glue area. The finished frame has a radius 15mm less than the top, and is 50mm deep. Using a 6mm plywood pattern cut to the correct radius, the router is employed to shape the segments.

I cut each piece with a jigsaw about 1mm oversize, and fixed the pattern with two 1/2in panel pins. The router is held in a table and, using a straight cutter and a close timber fence, replicas are made of the pattern which also doubles as a jig.

Final finishing of the frame is done by

der a ton

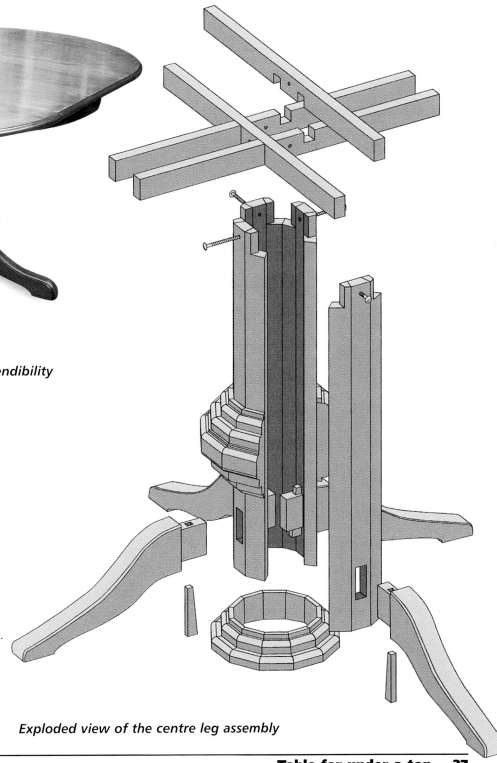

Invite some friends round for dinner to show off the table's extendibility

hand using a spokeshave, scraper and sandpaper.

Even more strength is added by mortice and tenoning two parallel rails into the circular frame about 750mm apart. These act as runners for the sliding top sections, and stand proud of the circular frame by 5mm, this being the amount that the table top edging overhangs the chipboard.

I routed grooves along the inside face of these rails to accommodate locating blocks screwed to the underside of the table tops.

The main support component of the subframe comprises four rails in the form of a cruciform half-lapped together in the centre like a noughts and crosses layout. An ovolo mould routed on the lower edge of the circular support frame completes the subframe.

Centre leg

I cut 12 pieces about 750mm long from the mahogany, then hand-planed both edges of each piece to an angle of 75°, so creating a hollow cylinder looking like a solid centre leg. With nowhere to cramp up, I glued

Exploded view of the centre leg assembly

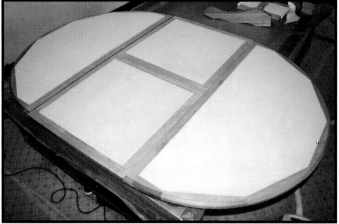

A folding extension piece is made in the same way as the round top

The outer subframe is built up from staggered segments for strength

Two parallel rails are built into the circular frame about 750mm apart for more strength and to act as runners for the sliding top sections

The centre leg is made up from 12 pieces with a 75° angle on each edge. Secret screws are used to hold them together while gluing

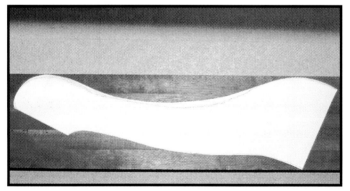

Use a paper pattern to mark out the legs

The hollow leg meant a tusk tenon joint with a difference could be used

them using the secret slot screw technique, *see panel.*

To ensure that the joints pull up really tight, give the screws a further half turn before gluing together. Using this method I built up sections of the leg in pairs and then effectively into two semi-circles. I was then able to plane any twist out of the two sections before completing the construction using the same jointing method.

Each facet of the leg is then planed to take out any overlap at the joints. The nom-inal overall diameter of the completed leg is 170mm, but I embellished mine with some built-up mouldings about half-way up and also around the base, *see panel.* Finally, the leg is cut to length and jointed to the cruciform section of the subframe by notch-ing out four corners and fitting four M8 coach bolts, *see panel.*

Feet

As the top is 1200mm in diameter, I decid-ed that the overall footprint dimension of the feet should be about 980mm. Allowing for the centre leg therefore, each foot had to be 405mm long plus an allowance for a tenon.

My paper pattern told me that I needed timber 125mm wide in order to produce the shape at its widest point. Back to my 45 by 25mm section material, and this time five pieces were glued together to make 125 by 45mm times 4 off.

It was then a matter of transferring the shape from the pattern to the wood and cut-

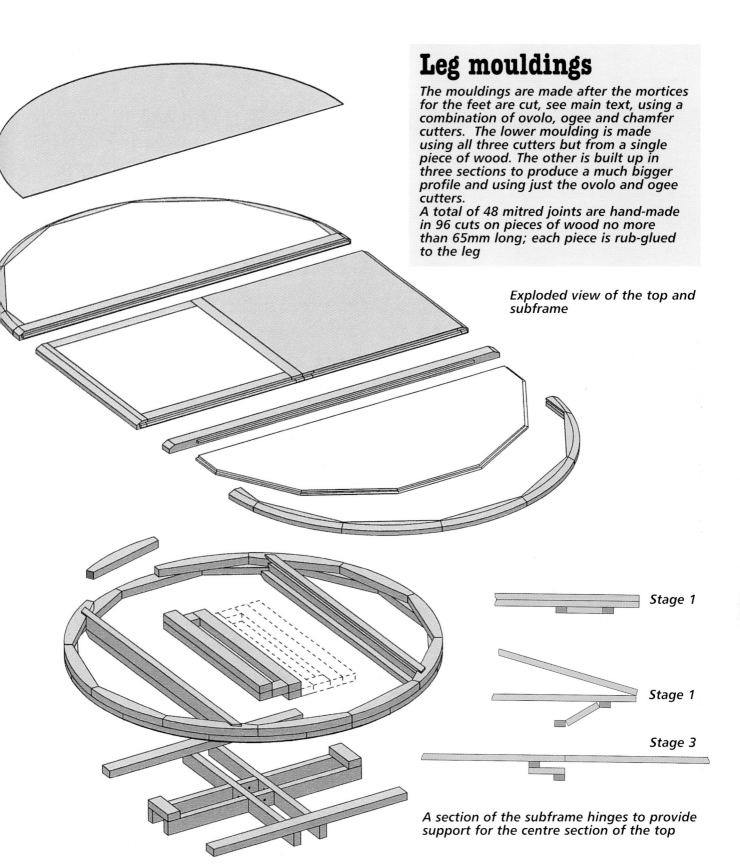

Leg mouldings

The mouldings are made after the mortices for the feet are cut, see main text, using a combination of ovolo, ogee and chamfer cutters. The lower moulding is made using all three cutters but from a single piece of wood. The other is built up in three sections to produce a much bigger profile and using just the ovolo and ogee cutters.

A total of 48 mitred joints are hand-made in 96 cuts on pieces of wood no more than 65mm long; each piece is rub-glued to the leg

Exploded view of the top and subframe

Stage 1

Stage 1

Stage 3

A section of the subframe hinges to provide support for the centre section of the top

ting it out on a friend's bandsaw. A bigger router than my 500W machine, with a ¹/₂in shank diameter, would have enabled me to finish the feet by attaching a plywood jig, as for the subframe perimeter rail, but I used a spokeshave and coarse sandpaper.

The hollow leg meant I was able to use a tusk tenon joint with a difference; instead of the wedge passing through the side of the tenon it has to go through its thickness, driven in from the base of the leg. To achieve this it was necessary to

make the tenon 25mm thick so that a 12mm-thick wedge would not significantly weaken it.

To complete the feet, I used the router to form two ovolo moulds on the top edges and the same cutter to simply radius the lower edges.

Assembly

The four feet, centre pedestal leg and subframe are fitted together as already described. For mobility, the joint

between the leg and subframe is not glued, allowing it to be dismantled. The centre top extension hinges in the middle to fold to half its 'in use' length.

Hafele produce a hinge which is installed from the edge and underside, so cannot be seen. This folding table hinge is available for three different thickness tops. In its open or 'in use' position, the centre top extension is supported on the same parallel rails as the main top.

In its closed or 'parked' position it

Mouldings made up using a variety of cutters are fitted to the centre leg above and below the legs

A section in the middle of the subframe hinges up to support the centre leaf

"The main support component of the subframe comprises four rails in the form of a cruciform half-lapped together in the centre like a noughts and crosses layout"

The base of the table assembled together

rests on the subframe. The task of transporting it between the two positions is performed using a double-hinged carrier frame, *see diagram*. Because the frame moves through 180° its dimension is half the distance that the top needs to move — in my case this was 150mm.

Finally, the two halves of the table top are held together in use with case clips fixed to the underside.

Finishing
The complete assembly is rubbed down with 80- followed by 100-grade production paper. The feet, centre leg and certain parts of the subframe are finished prior to final assembly to avoid dealing with awkward corners.

I decided to grain-fill the tops even though the cherry veneer is not particularly open-grained. For this I used Rustin's mahogany grain filler thinned with brown mahogany wood dye. I treated the whole table to one coat of brown mahogany wood dye, giving the top a further coat to balance the shading between the cherry and mahogany.

I then brush-applied three coats of Ronseal clear satin varnish to the leg and subframe assembly and six coats to the top.

I flatted each coat — allowing 24 hours to dry — with progressively finer production paper starting with 120- and finishing with 600-grade. Finally, I treated the top with Liberon fine paste wax polish which is difficult to burnish after 24 hours, but does produce a very tactile finish.

The table seats six people in normal use and 10 when fully extended, and cost less than £100 to make. ●

"The only way to achieve my aim was to go for veneer on a man-made board such as MDF or chipboard"

Secret slot screw technique
A screw with the head and shank sticking out about 12mm is fixed about 125mm from the end of each joint. The centres of the screws are then marked on the mating face of the adjoining piece. A hole is bored 12mm to the left or right of each mark to the same diameter as the screw head and to a depth of 12mm. A slot the same width as the screw shank is cut from the hole, towards and just past the original marks. The joint can then be fitted together dry to check for alignment simply by hammering one piece until the ends line up. Dismantle by tapping the other way.

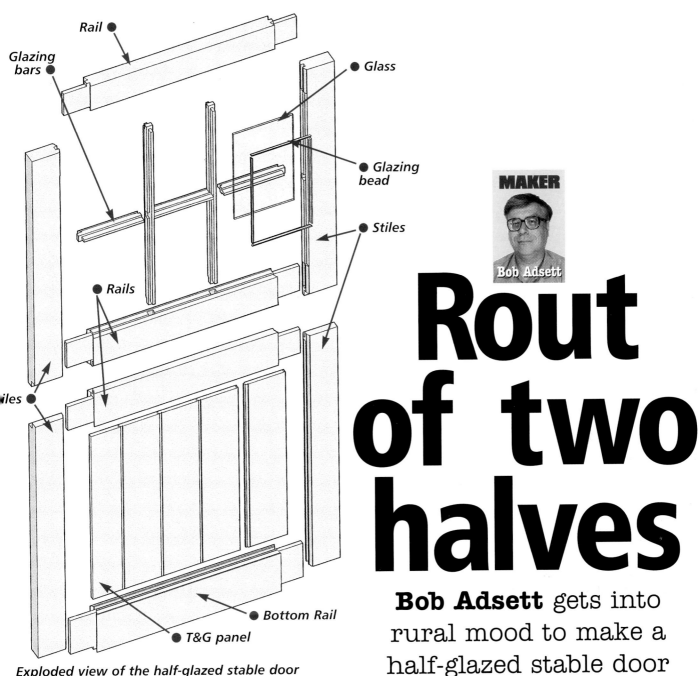

Rail ●

Glazing bars ●

● Glass

● Glazing bead

● Stiles

● Rails

iles ●

● Bottom Rail

● T&G panel

Exploded view of the half-glazed stable door

MAKER

Bob Adsett

Rout of two halves

Bob Adsett gets into rural mood to make a half-glazed stable door

This is a project for those who fancy one of those half-glazed stable doors which accessorise quaint country cottages, but are put off by the cost of having one custom-made.

This sort of door, made in separately opening halves, can be made inexpensively with standard-sized pine. Take care when selecting the wood from your local timber yard and look for boards that are as knot-free and tight-grained as possible.

After measuring the door aperture, carefully draw out a plan, making allowances for the overlap of the two halves and the overlap of the scribed joints; not doing so could result in the finished door being short on the width and height.

A powerful router with a ¹/₂in shank collet, inverted in a router table, is essential when machining the timber. I use a Ryobi RE 600N, one of the few routers that can be plunged so the collet is flush with the baseplate, providing useful extra reach.

Construction

The door frame is all constructed from ex 100 by 45mm (4 by 1³/₄in) for the rails and stiles except for the bottom rail that is from ex 140 by 45mm (5¹/₂ by 1³/₄in).

For strength, the mortice and tenon joints are made with haunches and the tenons are blind by about 10mm (³/₈in), i.e. they don't go right through the stiles so their end grain is protected from any adverse weather.

The mortices are 12.7mm (¹/₂in) thick and set 16mm (⁵/₈in) back from the face of the stiles. A rebate for the glass and its bead is cut to run flush with the back of the mortice, leaving approximately 16mm ((⁵/₈in) to balance the look of the door. Mark their positions, *see photo 1*, on the side rails and cut them using a 1¹/₂in diameter straight-fluted cutter, *see photo 2*, with a

60mm (2³/₈in) cutting length. This means that some hand-cutting of the mortice with a chisel is needed to attain the required depth.

The rails are all cut to length allowing for the tenon on each end, and then all the components are marked out, *see photo 3*.

A set-up piece is cramped to the bench with a couple of extra pieces on each side to support

Photo 1 Mortice marked out

Photo 2 Mortice cutting

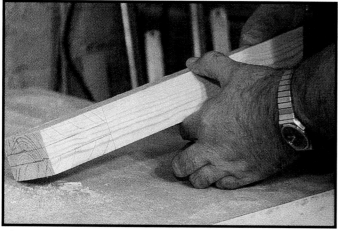
Photo 3 Tenon marked out

Photo 4 Cutting a tenon on one side

Photo 7 Rebating glazing bars

Photo 8 Moulding glazing bars

"For strength, all the mortices and tenons are made using haunches"

the baseplate, *see photo 4*. The router is set up with a straight cutter for tenoning and the test piece machined until the tenon fits the mortice. Then carry on to tenon all the components for the top and bottom door.

When the tenons are cut, set up the relevant part of the CMT window sash set in an inverted router and scribe the shoulders of the rails, *see photo 5*.

Glazing bars

Then scribe the ends of the glazing bars. The height is the same and only the depth needs changing to allow for their different tenon lengths. The ends of the glazing bars are located with stub tenons, *see photo 6*.

The scribed shoulders of all rails and the horizontal glazing bar are the same distance apart. This shoulder measurement is easily calculated and is the width of the door minus the width of the two stiles plus twice the 6.35mm (^{1}/4in) moulding measurement.

The four vertical glazing bars are then cut to length. Their

Tooling up

■ CMT Window sash set
■ CMT Multi groover set
■ CMT Bead cutter
■ Titan ^{1}/2in diameter by 60mm long straight cutter
■ Titan 1in diameter cutter
■ Ryobi RE 600N router with a ^{1}/2in collet mounted in a home-made table
■ Einhell EOF 850SP

size is calculated by measuring the height of the top half of the door, subtracting the width of the top and bottom rails then subtracting the width of the horizontal glazing bar.

To this measurement add four times the moulding depth of 6.35mm (^{1}/4in), then divide this figure by two to achieve the length of each vertical glazing bar (phew!— Ed.). Once cut to size their ends can also be scribed.

The top part of the door has a rebate for glass and bead but the bottom has a groove for a

Timber sizes

All stiles and top rails	100mm (4in) by 45mm (1^3/4in)
Bottom rail	140mm (5^1/2in) by 45mm (1^3/4in)
Glazing bars	32mm (1^1/4in) by 45mm (1^3/4in)
T&G boarding	12.5mm by 135mm (5^3/8in by ^{1}/2in)

Photo 5 *Scribing shoulder of tenon to fit moulding on sides*

Photo 6 *Scribing glazing bars with the same set-up*

Photo 9 *Grooving for panels in bottom half stile*

Photo 10 *Multi-grooving cutter set with spacers and four different sized grooving cutters*

Photo 11 *Grooving the edge of a T&G board*

Photo 12 *Cutting the tongue on the edge of the T&G board*

panel. Because of this it's easier to set up the moulding part of the window sash set to machine the moulding on all the components, *see photo 7*.

With this cutter installed, the glazing beads can also be machined, using only its curved part. To make these small section pieces safely, mould the edge of a board of the right thickness and then cut the mouldings off the edge.

The rebate part of the cutter is then used, *see photo 8*, to cut a rebate in the top door's rails, stiles and glazing bars. The groove in the bottom half of the door is created on the inside faces of the stiles and rails with a grooving cutter, *see photo 9*. It is set to cut a groove the same thickness as the panel, centrally in the door frame; two passes may be required.

Bottom panel

The panel is made up from tongue and grooved boards flush on the outside and with a bead formed on the joins inside. First, with a grooving cutter, *see photo 10*, machine a groove in one of the board edges, *see photo 11*, then on the other edge of the board rout one side of the tongue, turn the board over and rout the other, adjusting the depth of cut so that the tongue fits in the groove, *see photo 12*.

There is no need to machine the two outer edges of the assembled panel's end boards as

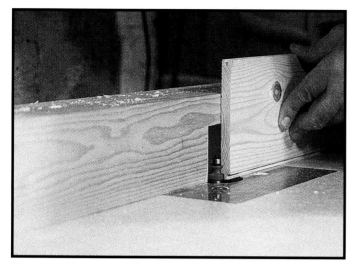

Photo 13 **Routing a bead on the inside of the T&G board**

The door seen from the outside

> "Bits of steel and tungsten rotating at 20,000rpm and leaving the router make a formidable projectile"

they are not seen. The bead on the face of the boards may be machined with them up flat against the fence of the router table, *see photo 13.*

Top frame

Before assembly dry-fit all components together to make sure everything fits.

Then glue and cramp up the assembly and check the diagonals for squareness. If out of square slacken the cramps then gently tap the corner of the longest measurement to nudge the frame square, retighten the clamps and check again.

Bottom frame

Again, check the components for fit then reassemble them with the panel in place and glue and cramp up, making sure that no glue gets into the panel groove. Use a silicon mastic in the groove to seal in the panel and allow it to move in expansion and contraction without splitting. The tongue and grooves panel can also be put together with mastic.

When dry, mark out for the rebates on the overlap of the top and bottom door sections, *see photo 14,* using a hand-held router clamped with a straight-edge to the door; cut out the rebates in a number of passes.

Beads and drips

Cut and mitre the glazing beads to fit with the use of a mitre saw or mitre block and tenon saw; small pins will hold them and the glass in place.

The door should be fitted into its frame before any of the drip pieces are fitted — these non-routed components were inexpensively bought from a timber mill.

Clean up and sand the door, then finish it to match the rest of the woodwork on your house. ●

Photo 14 **Rebating the two halves of the door**

Fine door, fine view

Wooden battens hold the door halves together while marking out and fitting

MAKER
Colin Eden-Eadon

Colin Eden-Eadon fits the stable door made by Bob Adsett and featured in the previous article

Make mine a double

Only the paint was holding our old stable door together. Serving as our front door, in places it was so thin you could poke your finger through. As our house has low ceilings and only two windows in the living room area, a door which lets in some extra light is very welcome.

Being in two halves, stable doors can be tricky to fit, tending to bind on each other if fitted singly. The answer is temporarily to make them one by nailing or screwing two strips of wood on each side of the door; fill in the resulting holes before painting.

With the halves married up they can be tried for fit. Mine went in first time— well done Bob!

Because this is a replacement door I marked the hinge sockets off the originals on the door frame, and then marked their positions onto the door.

Hinge jig
The hinge jig uses a 17mm guide bush, a 10mm cutter, and a simple template made to suit. The margin between guide bush and

cutter is 3.5mm in this instance. This jig is simply made from 6mm MDF cut out on a bandsaw, allowing 3.5mm larger than the hinge all round; a fence screwed to it allows it to be clamped to the door.

Slotting the screw holes would produce an adjustable jig, and, for a posh job, clear plastic could be substituted for the MDF.

The router cutter depth is taken directly off the hinges; a fine adjuster takes the awkwardness out of setting up small depths.

After clamping the jig in place I routed the sockets, then cleaned out the corners with a chisel before fitting the hinges and screwing them in place.

Because adjustment will probably be needed, don't waste time and effort putting all the screws in at this stage.

I usually put two in each hinge and then the same into the door frame. Having temporarily put the door on, check it for fit and adjust where necessary before finally screwing into place.

Lastly, the dripbars are attached; the bottom one must be fettled a little to allow for the swing of the door. ●

▲ **Hinge jig clamped to the door**

◀ **Setting the router up to the hinge depth**

Burning bright

Anthony Bailey
makes a candle sconce
to create the mood for
romantic evenings

THERE'S nothing so romantic as candlelight, and this delightful, traditional-style candle sconce will add a charming touch to any room, and that extra something to dinner parties, or simple, cosy nights in. It uses little in the way of materials and the slim mirror behind the candle adds another dimension of light.

> "It uses little in the way of materials and the slim mirror behind the candle adds another dimension of light"

Template

First, mark out on a piece of 6 or 9mm (¼ or ⁷⁄₁₆ in) MDF, the complete outline` of the sconce, plus the mirror aperture and the hanging slot, as in the drawing – 6mm (¼ in) is better if your guide bush is short enough – I ground mine down – as the hanging slot needs a narrow cutter which is short, so maximum cutter projection is needed.

Ensure the design is perfectly symmetrical from side to side – use compasses for the curves and setting-out lines to ensure complete accuracy, or do as I did, and stick a photocopy of the design directly on the template board.

It is possible to machine just about every part of the template with a router on the

▶ *An attractive candle sconce made from pine*

▲ *Rout the sides of the template on a router table*

Shoulders

The two radiused shoulders can be made using a 19mm (¾in) cutter and the mitre fence. You will need to take care, and remember that the leading radius is pushed onto the cutter while the trailing one has to be dropped on, so that the correct direction of cut is maintained. It sounds tricky but this kind of semi-freehand shaping can be done on the table, provided it is in small passes, gradually moving up to the line.

Once all major template shaping is done, use a jigsaw, or bandsaw if you have one, and cut the more complex shapes, cutting close to, but not up to, the line. Now take a half-round, coarse wood file and clean all the shapes up, taking care that you stop on the marked-out lines.

Keyhole

The keyhole is interesting to do – the guide bush cut-out is rounded out to size to create the shape at the bottom, with a change of cutters to create the different shapes that result.

The idea is to use a 3.2mm (⅛in) cutter for the slot and a 6.3mm (¼in) cutter for the round, using the same guide bush for both – I used a 17mm (¹¹⁄₃₂in) guide bush, but you may need to experiment. The result is the proper inverted keyhole shape on the finished article.

The sconce template, once it is made, can be used time and again to produce as many sconces as you want.

table, but this is not practical, so stick with doing the main shapes – the straight edges can be routed against the fence as well as the slots for the mirror cut-out, although you will need to stop short of the corners on this. The major curve at the top, which must be

neat, can be done with an inboard trammel on a sub-base which involves bolting a piece of 6mm (¼in) MDF onto your router base and threading a piece of studding into a slightly smaller hole, drilled at the appropriate radius point, away from the cutter.

▲ *The mirror cut-out on the template is also a simple job with a pair of straight cuts*

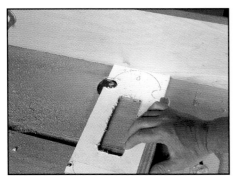

▲ *Use the mitre fence to create the radiused shoulders*

▲*The large radius on the top of the template is made using a simple jig*

290mm
(11⁷/₁₆in)

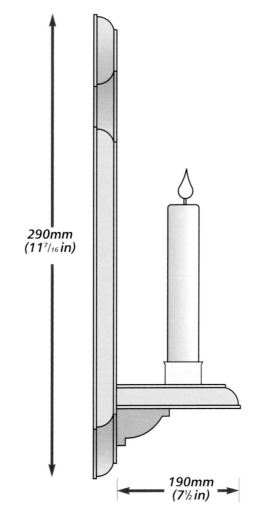

129mm
(5¹/₁₆in)

190mm
(7½in)

"The keyhole is interesting to do – the guide bush cut-out is rounded out to size to create the shape at the bottom, with a change of cutters to create the different shapes that result"

Timber

Select a piece of pine with as few knots as possible, and as flat as you can find, measuring approximately 150mm (6in) across by 19mm (¾in) thick – the prepared size will of course be slightly less thick at about 16mm (⅝in).

Mark out the shape, over-size by a couple of millimetres, then cut to the line. Ensure that any knots in the wood are suitably placed out of harm's way, and then pin the template to the reverse side.

Routing

Fit a top-bearing guided straight cutter into your router, after installing the machine in the router table. Make sure the cutter is sharp and when trimming don't

▼ *The finished template with cutters and shortened guidebush for cutting the hanging slot*

▲ *Fix the template to a suitable piece of pine and run around it with a top-bearing straight cutter*

linger, especially on curves, as burning will result.

Use a lead-in point or finger which acts as a kind of point-fence, reducing the risk of kickback. Work steadily around the perimeter of the work until it is complete, then remove the lead-in point, drop the workpiece over the cutter, and trim up the mirror hole.

Remember that because you are machining the internal cut, you will be running against the other side of the cutter in order that the wood is still fed into the advancing cutter blades – rather than backfeeding.

▲ *Turn the sconce over to apply the moulding on the face*

▲ *A flatbit is used to make the recess for the candle holder*

Ovolo

Once the initial shaping has been done, remove the template and swap cutters for a 9.5mm (⅜in) ovolo cutter – this is effectively a roundover cutter fitted with a small bearing which gives a slight step.

Rather than machining the complete

"Take the finished article to the glaziers and get them to cut the mirror to fit which they will do at little cost"

ovolo cut in one scorching pass, set the cutter down for a lighter pass, then do a test cut for the full profile, and finally machine the external profile.

The centre hole is for the mirror, so a smaller 6.3mm (¼in) ovolo is prescribed to keep the full ovolo profile, once the mirror rebate has been machined out to take a piece of 3mm (⅛in) mirror glass.

Fit the guide bush and freehand machine the keyhole using the two different cutters, taking care not to let the larger cutter move up into the slot area at the top.

Now remove the template and fit a 10mm (⅜in) bearing guided rebate cutter in the table and rebate the back of the sconce so that the slot will accommodate the mirror without removing the step on the ovolo.

Candle holder

The piece for the candle to fit into needs to be cut overlength and a template piece marked out to take the brass candle insert. I used a 17mm (¹¹⁄₃₂in) guide bush and a 6.3mm bit – unfortunately the 1¼in flatbit I used gave a slightly oversized hole, a 30mm flatbit would have been better.

Pin the template on, beyond the point where the timber will be sawn off, thus avoiding visible pin holes. Now use the

9.5mm (⅜in) ovolo cutter to shape the end and two sides, and cut to length.

Drill two holes for screws through the back of the sconce and use the screw points to spike the positions on the candle-piece, then drill pilot holes in it and glue and screw it on.

The bracket underneath, I shaped on the bandsaw, although a jigsaw or hand coping-saw will do as well. Carefully clean it up with a wood file and some abrasive, then lightly glue, rub gently into position, and allow to dry.

Once the glue has set, varnish the whole piece carefully and flat the varnish with lubricating paper between coats. The brass insert can then be screwed or epoxy resined into place. Take the finished article to the glaziers and get them to cut the mirror to fit which they will do at little cost.

Finally plug and screw the sconce to the wall in a suitable place – sit down to dinner and bask in the gentle reflected glory of candlelight! ●

Candlestick inserts, gold plated, brass, and silver plated, are available in packs of four from:
Craft Supplies Ltd, *The Mill, Millers' Dale, Buxton, Derbyshire SK17 8SN.*
Tel: 01298 871636, fax: 01298 872263.

Tooling up

- ■ **Top bearing-guided straight cutter**
- ■ **Small straight cutter**
- ■ **¼in straight cutter**
- ■ **Small ovolo cutter**
- ■ **Large ovolo cutter**

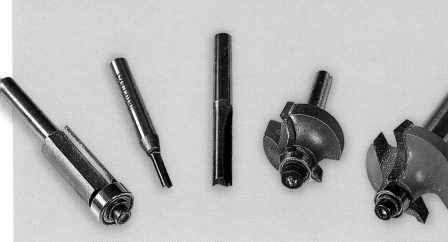

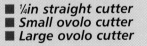

▲ *Your local glazier will cut a suitably sized piece of mirror*

In the frame

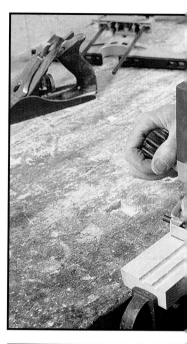

Don't be fooled by the apparent simplicity of **Roger Smith's** picture or mirror frame – its square-cut joints require precision

I HAVE always believed that making something simple but well is more desirable than making something complicated that doesn't quite come up to scratch.

This picture/mirror frame is constructed using basic techniques. While it requires few tools it will test the maker as it needs accurate square-cut joints.

Its clean lines create a different, and in my opinion preferable, impression to that

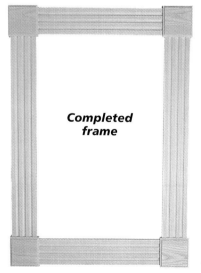

Completed frame

seen in a frame with mitred corners.

Any timber can be used but I chose ash (*Fraxinus sp*) as hardwoods tend to give a crisper finish. Routing softwood can produce woolly surfaces and excess sanding removes edge definition.

If you have no facility for machining the wood to size, standard prepared timber from a merchant can be used, with the dimensions of the frame altered to suit.

Routing flutes

The first job is to rout the flutes in the rails with a 10mm diameter radius cutter. Leave the pieces at least 100mm (4in) over length to allow for the possibility of the router dipping at the end of a workpiece.

If a bench with a tail vice is not available, the workpiece can be held with a sash cramp in a vice.

Rout the central flute first, then machine the other two flutes by working from either edge. The flutes must be equally spaced. Practise on a piece of spare wood of the

Tooling up

Cutters used: 8mm radius cutter; 13mm diameter bearing guided cove cutter; 9mm straight; 12mm straight.

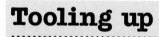

same dimensions as the actual frame.

If you are in any doubt about the accuracy of the stock, rout the flutes with the fence kept against the same edge.

With any routing process avoid stopping during a cut as burn marks can only be removed by tiresome and excessive sanding.

Cutting rebate

The next step is to cut the rebate to take the glass or picture. Decide on the dimensions, and set the fence and a depth stop. Taking small cuts, rout the rebate, adjusting the router to cut deeper with each pass until the correct depth is achieved.

The sides can now be cut to length – the most critical phase of the project. A tenon saw could be used, but the ends might not end up square. So instead of a hand saw I would revert to the trusty router.

Cramp all four pieces of wood and a backing piece together side-by-side and mark where the timber is to be machined to length.

Measure the distance from the edge of the router baseplate to the cutting edge of the straight-fluted cutter. Then cramp a batten across the side rails at this distance back from the mark on the workpieces, start up the router and trim up the ends.

If this method of squaring

1 Routing
flutes –
using sash
cramp in
vice

2 Routing
rebate

3 Cutting
the edge
moulding
on corner
blocks

4 Routing
loose-
tongue
slots

up the ends is chosen, do it before the flutes and rebate are cut to avoid breakout.

Corner blocks

Square and accurate inner faces are vital to the successful assembly of the four corner blocks to the four rails.

Any of the above methods can be used to cut them square and to size, taking extra care to hold the small pieces securely. Then apply the edge moulding.

Clamp them securely into a vice and keep the router base firmly in contact with the block, routing around the edge with either a 13mm diameter bearing guided cove

"With any routing process avoid stopping during a cut as burn marks can only be removed by tiresome and excessive sanding"

bit or a 13mm diameter radius cutter used in conjunction with a fence.

Cut the end-grain first and then proceed in an anti-clockwise direction to eliminate breakout. The same cutter used on the flutes may be used on the blocks, but the decoration it creates may look rather small.

Laying the eight components on the bench will now reveal the overall effect and tell you how accurate your cutting has been.

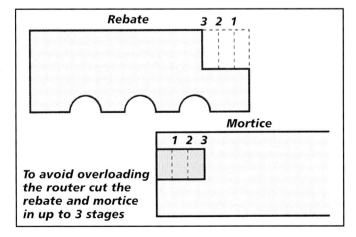

Rebate   3 2 1

Mortice

1 2 3

To avoid overloading
the router cut the
rebate and mortice
in up to 3 stages

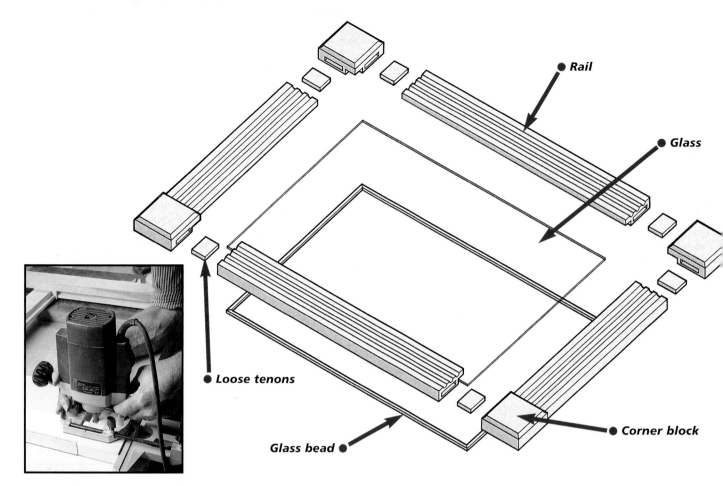

▲ Routing out corners

▲ Exploded view of picture/mirror frame

Labels on exploded view: Rail, Glass, Corner block, Glass bead, Loose tenons

Loose-tongues

The loose-tongue joints at each corner require slots routed approximately 40mm (1½in) long by 9mm (³⁄₈in) wide by 15mm (⁵⁄₈in) deep. I used a 9mm straight flute cutter but 6 or 12mm cutters or their imperial equivalents would do the job just as well.

Routing mortices for the loose-tongues will require additional support for the router fence and base as the supporting surface on the edge of the stock is small. Clamping a longer piece of wood by the side of the workpiece will do the job.

The loose-tongue for the joint can be made of solid wood or ply, but if solid wood is used make sure the grain direction runs across the joint – a tongue that is not cross-grained will have limited strength.

Gluing up

Glue and clamp two of the corner blocks to one side rail, then the other two to the opposite side rail, making sure the grain directions of the corner blocks line up.

When the glue is dry the two remaining sides can be glued and sash-cramped into position to complete the frame.

The gluing operation is one that can go badly wrong if the side rails are not central in the corner blocks. Make sure the blocks overhang the sides by equal amounts otherwise the frame will not end up square.

Aim to have no glue oozing from the joint. The only real way to keep a joint of this nature looking good is by not having to remove excess glue with chisel or damp rag.

Extending rebate

The picture/mirror rebate will need extending into the corner blocks. To rout this, turn the frame on its back and fix some packing pieces with double-sided tape into the step, so providing the router fence with a better bearing surface.

After machining out the corner, the small amount of remaining wood can be chiselled square.

Finishing

The completed frame is now ready to be finished. I favour lacquering to retain the wood's original colour, or, if a darker surface is desired, oiling.

Danish oil is attractive, especially when applied over a coat of boiled linseed. The linseed makes it easier to apply subsequent layers of oil more evenly.

A steamy bathroom calls for a more durable polyurethane finish. Remember that one coat too few often looks better than one coat too many.

The size of the beading that retains the picture or mirror is largely determined by the thickness of the glass and the depth of the rebate. I prefer fixing it into the frame with screws, but pins are acceptable.

Fixing

Fixing the frame to a wall can be achieved in a couple of ways. Picture wire strung between two eye screws on the back of the frame and hung from a screw in the wall is preferable for a picture.

A mirror is best fixed flat, secured by brass mirror plates that screw into both the back of the frame and then the wall. ●

Tooling up

Cutters used

This simple design of frame is attractive and is easy to make any size by just making the side rails longer or shorter.
I worked to the following:

Side rails: 70 by 25mm (2½ by 1in) – cut 100mm (4in) longer than required to allow for routing the flutes

Corner blocks: 83 by 83 by 32mm (3¼ by 3¼ by 1¼in)

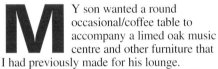
Bill Cain makes a round table to complement other limed oak pieces

Stock answer

MY son wanted a round occasional/coffee table to accompany a limed oak music centre and other furniture that I had previously made for his lounge.

He wanted its size, height, edge moulding and finish to match the other items, but these 'customer driven' parameters may obviously be varied to suit your requirements.

Materials, methods

A visit to Interesting Timbers, the yard at Emborough, near Bath, run by David and Catherine Simmonds, secured good quality, sensibly priced sawn/kilned English oak (*Quercus robur*) boards for the table top. Material for the legs and frame came from stock left over from previous jobs.

The construction methods chosen were all straightforward and, as always, dictated by the range and type of equipment available in the workshop. For example, I have a bench morticer, but the mortices have been

"If you pull the boards together with cramps to close a small gap then they are almost sure to open up at a later date"

produced with a router to show how versatile they can be.

Table top

Since this is the surface most seen, care needs to be taken to select the best and/or most interesting areas of the boards before cutting. Surface plane to thickness and cut to length – I always leave plenty on the length just in case a 'snipe' results when thicknessing.

Arrange the boards, *see fig 1*, and mark the edges to be jointed. Plane or rout the edges true, ensuring that they are square to the face with 100% edge contact over the full length of the joint faces. If you pull the

boards together with cramps to close a small gap then they are almost sure to open up at a later date.

Using a size 20 biscuit and PVA adhesive, biscuit-joint the edges together to form the top. For this task a Trend biscuit jointer cutter in an ELU 177E router, inverted in a table, works well, but keep your fingers well clear of the unguarded cutter.

There are many ways of cutting circular table tops, but I prefer to use a bandsaw and table-mounted router with a template, rather than a freehand router on the end of a long trammel bar, but go with whatever method you feel happy about.

▲ *Fig 1 Exploded view of table*

Follow this method:
1. Manufacture a 6mm thick by 700mm (27½in) diameter MDF template using the

▼ *Photo 2 Cramp a strip of thick MDF to the bandsaw ...*

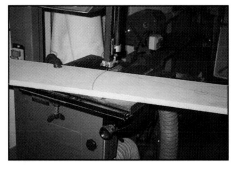

bandsaw set-up shown, *see photos 2 and 3*. This employs the use of a remote centre pin, in an MDF jig or board clamped to the bandsaw table. Set the pin at a radius of 350mm (13¾in) from the cutting edge of the bandsaw blade and rotate the work that is to be cut.
2. Sand the edge of the MDF template to remove all bandsaw marks. These will be amplified when using this edge as a guide while routing the edge of the table top material, and could result in a rippled edge if the template is not smooth.
3. Using the same method as described above, but with the remote centre set at a radius of 351mm (13⅞in), bandsaw the assembled table top boards to cut a circle of 702mm (27⅝in) diameter – so leaving a 1mm (½2in) routing cut

for final clean-up to the 700mm (27⅝in) diameter of the template.

▼ *Photo 3 ... then place a centre pin at the required diameter and cut the template to size*

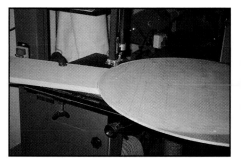

▲ *Photo 4 screw the template to the table top and rout the edge all round*

Photo 6 Mount the legs in the lathe and mark the extent of the turning

4. Screw the MDF template to the bottom face of the top and, with a bearing-guided template profile cutter, rout in a single full-depth pass to the 700mm (27%₆in) diameter of the template. Sand the edge, *see photo 4.*

While the above may sound a bit long-winded, I find it quick, safe and accurate. It does not overload the router/cutter and, even executed in oak, permits a single, continuous high-speed, full-depth pass to produce a good ripple-free finish.

5. Remove the template, sand the edge and, with a bearing-guided moulding cutter apply your choice of edge moulding.

6. Finish-sand all surfaces.

Legs (4 off)

Prepare material to finish size 50 by 50mm (2 by 2in) and cut to length at 370mm (14%₆in). Mark out and cut the mortices in each leg, using a bench router, *see photo 5.*

Mark the centre at each end of the work and turn the legs between centres to embrace your chosen design. Either turn them by hand in a lathe, *see photos 6 and 7*, with a router in a home-made or shop-bought router lathe or even rout an interesting lateral design on the square leg, such as a stop chamfer. Finish-sand.

Photo 7 Turn them to the desired shape

Side rails (4 off)

Prepare material to finish section 75 by 24mm (3 by 1in) and cut to length at 350mm (13¾in) plus the length of the two tenons. Cut the tenons by your preferred method.

Photo 5 Mortice the legs, using a side fence on the router and an end stop on the bench

Using lime paste

Instead of using liming wax, I have always relied on Fiddes Lime Paste. In a process of trial and error I have established that satisfactory results can be gained by the following technique:

1. Finish-sand down to 400 grit wet and dry. Care is paramount as even the smallest circular orbital sanding marks will be emphasised by the liming and will show through the finish coating.

2. Clean out the grain with a stiff bronze wire brush.

3. Mask off the faces to be jointed, so preventing contamination with lime paste/finish coating.

4. Apply liming paste with a slightly damp rag, scrubbing it well into the grain; do not allow it to dry too much before removing the excess with clean, damp cloths. Allow the surface to dry and sand lightly to 400 grit to remove the raised grain.

5. Seal the limed face with a spray coat of clear lacquer, such as Humbrol Crystal Clear Acrylic Coating.

This product is acetone-based, so allow a minimum of 36 hours before over-coating to permit the solvent to evaporate fully. Failure to allow suffi-cient time can result in a chemical reaction with a white spirit-based varnish top coating. It will bubble and end up a sticky mess – I know because I've been there!

The use of a sealer coat prevents the lime paste from being drawn out of the grain when the finishing coat is being brushed on.

6. De-nib the sealer coat, using 800 grit paper, and apply the finish coating. I used two coats, sanded in between, of Fiddes Clear Satin Glaze. This provides a clear finish with very little 'yellowing' effect. Lightly sand and wax.

Photo 8 First rout the tenons to width

"I have found that the bandsaw with a fine tooth blade and slow feed gives quick, repeatable and accurate results with very little clean up/paring required"

I use a router set-up, *see photos 8 and 9*, and first cut the tenons to width and then turn the side rails on edge to cut the shoulders.

Rout the cove edge mouldings along the length of the rails and the 8 by 8mm (⅜ by ⅜in) slot into which the top securing 'buttons' engage.

Sand all surfaces. Manufacture the 8 off top securing buttons, *dimensions shown in fig 2*.

Photo 9 Then turn the rails to cut the shoulders

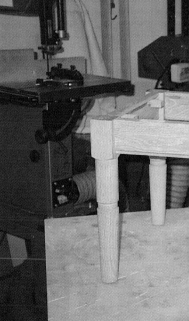

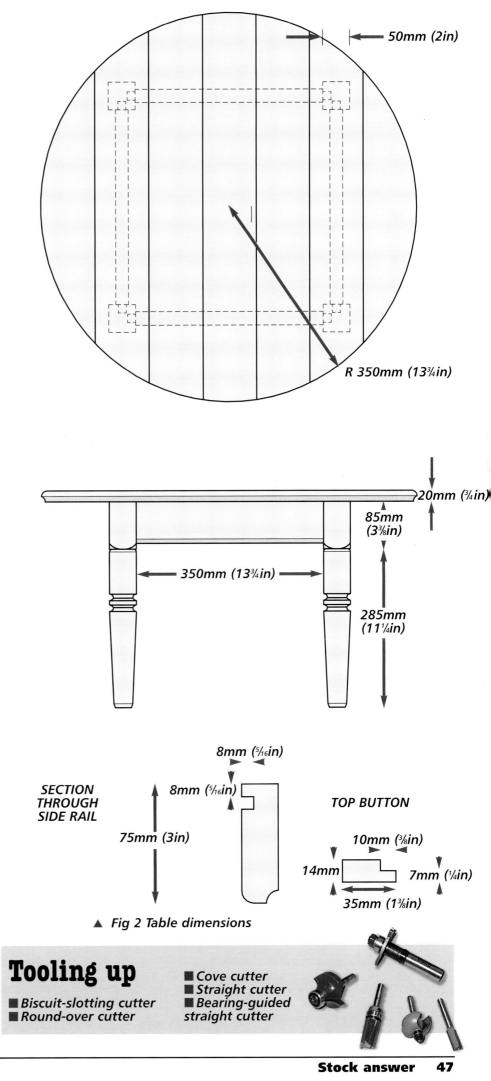

"Even executed in oak, this method permits a single, continuous high-speed, full-depth pass to produce a good ripple-free finish"

Assembly

Normally the frame would be assembled and glued at this stage. Since, however, it is to receive a limed finish, go for a trial fit, mark all parts, disassemble and apply the liming paste and final finish to the detail parts, *see panel.*

This method prevents any unsightly build-up of lime or varnish around the joints and, since the water-based liming process will raise the grain, it also makes for better sanding.

Finishing

For many of us, finishing is 'make or break time'. I have to admit that while finishing is not my favourite activity, it does sometimes present new challenges to be overcome, *see panel.*

Final assembly

Remove the masking from the joints and glue up the frame with PVA.

Position the frame to the underside of the top and secure with the 8 off 'buttons', using brass screws. ●

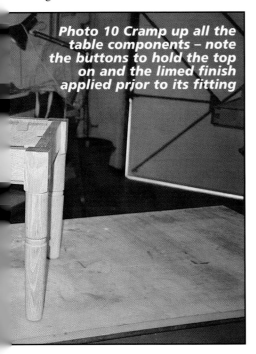

Photo 10 Cramp up all the table components – note the buttons to hold the top on and the limed finish applied prior to its fitting

R 350mm (13¾in)

50mm (2in)

20mm (¾in)

85mm (3⅜in)

350mm (13¾in)

285mm (11¼in)

SECTION THROUGH SIDE RAIL

8mm (⁵⁄₁₆in)

8mm (⁵⁄₁₆in)

75mm (3in)

TOP BUTTON

10mm (⅜in)

14mm

7mm (¼in)

35mm (1⅜in)

▲ *Fig 2 Table dimensions*

Tooling up

- **Biscuit-slotting cutter**
- **Round-over cutter**
- Cove cutter
- Straight cutter
- Bearing-guided straight cutter

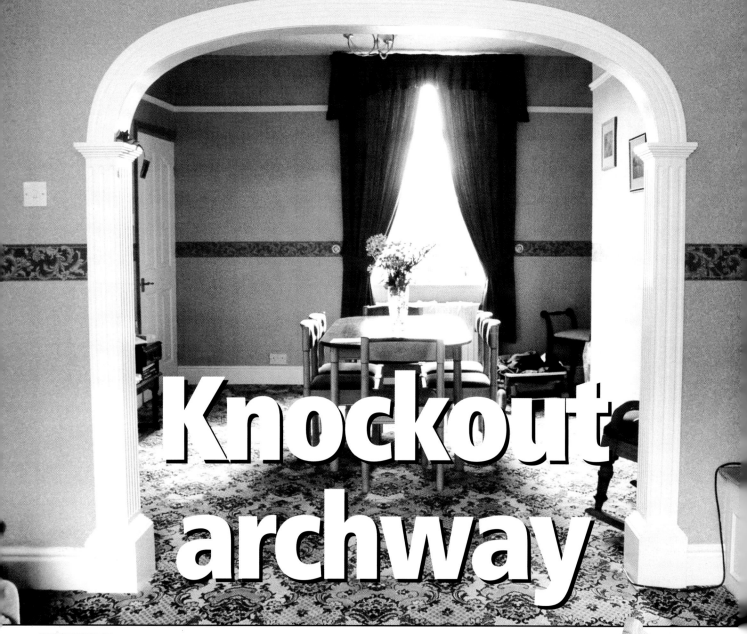

Knockout archway

Lee Ninham tidies up a demolished wall with a decorative arch and columns

AFTER knocking out part of my middle wall to create a through room, I was left with an alarmingly large hole which needed something special doing to it to finish it off, instead of just leaving it with a plain 'plastered-up' squared-edge finish.

After some deliberation, I decided that some fluted columns for the walls and a fancy arch had to be made to complete the job in a manner that justified my router's place in the workshop.

I had already installed a steel girder over the opening, with timber battens bolted onto it to allow me to fix my arch.

The opening left after this was two metres wide and the wall, being only one brick thick, measured 135mm (5⁵⁄₁₆in), so the channels making up the columns had to be a snug fit on this.

Columns

The job of building my architectural feature began by making the columns using a length of 19 by 150mm (¾ by 6in) P.A.R. (planed all round) softwood.

The flutes are marked out and equally spaced across its width, four or five to suit. Then, with a 20mm core box cutter in the router and using the side-fence, I cut the flutes with two passes of the machine finally set to the required depth of 5mm (³⁄₁₆in).

> **"The job of building my architectural feature began by making the columns"**

▲ *An architectural arch tidies up a demolished wall*

▶ *Pic 2 The skirting is made up from three components – note the packing piece*

Pic 3 Angles are cut on the ends of the arch components and biscuit slots cut

To limit the length of the flutes, a small batten is fixed to the timber using double-sided tape.

This is positioned after calculating the edge-of-cutter to edge-of-router baseplate distance, and also serves to make sure all the ends of the flutes line up.

Make sure that the pieces of wood for the columns are a little overlength so they can be trimmed to size.

Rout a small rebate on the back edges of the centre board, the purpose being to house the two side pieces. For this, a straight cutter is used and is set up to cut 5mm (³⁄₁₆in) deep and the side-fence set so a 15mm (⁵⁄₈in) cut is made – the thickness of the side piece.

The same process is then used to cut the three flutes in the 115mm (4½in) wide sides although it must be noted that the thickness of the front must be allowed for when marking out the spacings of the flutes, *see fig 1*. Also, don't forget that the bottom of the column has a 240mm (9½in) high skirting and moulding.

Tooling up

Router:
- 20mm core box cutter
- 13mm core box cutter
- 5mm core box cutter
- A straight-fluted cutter
- Bearing-guided trimmer
- Mitre saw
- Masonry drill

"I arranged them in a different order to produce a more varied pattern of moulding"

▶ *Fig 1 The centre board is housed on the edges to accept the column sides*

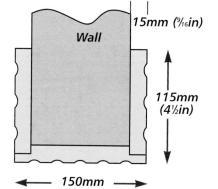

Wall

15mm (⁹⁄₁₆in)

115mm (4½in)

150mm (5⁷⁄₈in)

Pic 4 When the glue is dry mark out the arches with a template ...

P.A.T.

R.H.

Pic 5 ... then cut out using a jigsaw

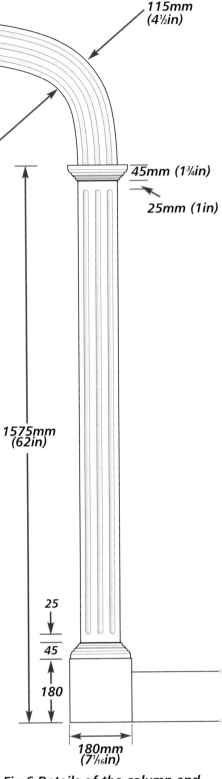

115mm (4½in)

45mm (1¾in)

25mm (1in)

1575mm (62in)

25

45

180

180mm (7¹⁄₁₆in)

▲ Fig 6 Details of the column and arch fluting

Top, bottom mouldings

The next job is to machine the mouldings that are fitted to the top and bottom of the columns.

For the skirting I used three separate pieces of wood, two moulded pieces built up on top of the 180mm (7¹⁄₁₆in) wide plain bottom, giving the appearance of a deep 240mm (9½in) skirting, *see pic 2*.

Using a Roman ogee cutter on the 15 by 35mm (9⁄₁₆ by 1⅜in) pieces of timber – long enough to go around three sides of the column four times and allowing for mitres – I routed a moulding on their face side, one further piece, the same length, being moulded on the edge.

This was so that I could arrange them in a different order to produce a more varied pattern of moulding.

Not having a router table, I can only guess that it would be a little easier when having to run off a few lengths of moulding; nevertheless I now had three sets of mouldings for the job, which I

then glued together and cramped up.

Once the glue is dry the mitres can be cut and the pieces fitted around the columns using a packing piece behind the wide part.

> "I first had to decide on the exact shape of the arch, so with the aid of a piece of hardboard I tried a few different shapes and held them in place"

Pic 7 Cut guidebush slots in the template for routing the flutes

> "I would normally have used dowels for these joints but I thought it was time I tried using biscuits – and I am pleased I did"

Pic 8 The three parts of the skirting are mitred and fitted to the columns

Arch

I first had to decide on the exact shape of the arch, so with the aid of a piece of hardboard I tried a few different shapes and held them in place. Eventually one was drawn that looked right and everybody was happy with.

This was then transferred to thin MDF, to be used as a pattern for routing the arch shape. Make sure that the curve is smooth and even, using a spokeshave,

Pic 9 Nail on some 19mm blocks to the inside edges of the arch before fixing

files and sandpaper.

The arch consists of a softwood front and back with a thin plywood skin bent around the inside curve to complete.

The softwood pieces are made from 18 by 180mm (¾ by 7in) P.A.R., but as there is a severe curve to get around they must be made in sections to economise on wood.

The sections are made up by cutting the ends at an angle. This is determined by placing the pattern on top of two pieces and

moving them until the curve is covered.

Cut the angles then, with a biscuit joint slotting cutter fitted in the router, all the joint slots are machined, see pic 3.

I would normally have used dowels for these joints but I thought it was time I tried using biscuits – and I am pleased I did as this method is much faster and more accurate, giving a stronger joint. No more fiddling with dowels for me!

All the sections are then glued, cramped up and left until completely dry.

Place the pattern on top of one of the arch assemblies and mark out the shape, see pic 4, then, with a jigsaw, carefully cut about 3mm (⅛in) outside the lines, see pic 5.

Attach the pattern to the arch with screws – the holes can be filled later – then, with a trimming cutter, rout all the arch pieces to shape.

When this is done, smooth the edges and make the faces flat.

To give an interesting detail, the three flutes are different sizes, 20mm, 13mm and 5mm, which means using three core box cutters set to cut 2 to 3mm (¹⁄₁₆ to ⅛in) deep, see fig 6.

I routed the 20mm flute by running the side-fence against the outside curve of the arch, but abandoned this approach as it was difficult to get a smooth cut.

On the template, mark out slots for the two other flutes; I made them 17mm wide to suit my guidebush, see pic 7, making sure they were perfectly smooth and a constant width.

The actual routing of the slots proved to be the simplest part of the job.

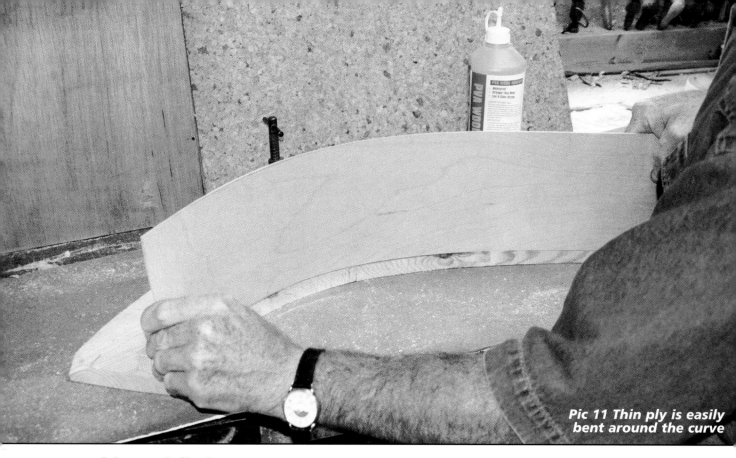

Pic 11 Thin ply is easily bent around the curve

Assembly and fitting

The columns are made up first, the two side boards fitting into the rebate on the back of the centre board. These are glued and pinned together and, when dry, the columns can be fixed to the wall.

Find the best places to drill holes in the columns so they key into a brick, then drill through with a masonry drill and insert Rawlplugs. I attached them with 50mm (2in) long countersunk screws and plugs.

The three pieces of the skirting were fitted in sequence, *see pic 8*; the 180mm plain board is mitred, glued and nailed on the bottom of the columns, after first fixing spacers or packing pieces to allow for the 32mm-thick moulding.

The two mouldings are then cut to size, mitred on my indispensable mitre saw, glued and pinned to the top of the plain board. The top of the column is then finished off by attaching the two moulding parts.

Lastly, the arch pieces are fitted on the top of the columns and attached to the wall. To allow fixing of the ply on the underneath of the arch I nailed on some 19mm blocks to the inside edges of the arch before fixing, *see pic 9*.

Both arch sides are then screwed to the wall using screws and Rawlplugs just above the columns. On the long span they are screwed to laths which I had already fixed to the supporting girder, *see fig 10*.

The 2mm-thick strips of ply can then be easily bent to shape and tacked in place to complete the construction of the archway, *see pic 11*.

The last job is to carefully fill in all the screw and nail holes before letting my wife loose with the paint brush! ●

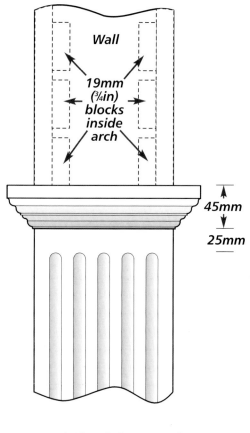

▲ Fig 10 Cross-section through arch

▼ Detail of the moulding on the top of the column

▼ Right-hand side of the archway finished and painted

Face value

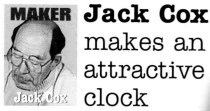
MAKER **Jack Cox** makes an attractive clock face with the help of his pivot-frame

Jack Cox

READERS who are unfamiliar with the Trend pivot-frame router jig may be a little surprised to know that this clock face can be made almost entirely with it – the only exception being the segmentation of the basic timber groundwork, which is not a necessary requirement, if a sufficiently large piece of timber is available to begin with.

Pivot-frame

The pivot-frame jig rotates around a flat disc, called a primary disc, which can be made from a sheet of plywood or MDF.

The router can be positioned and locked on the guide rods to cut a circle, or part-circle, of any desired diameter in the workpiece, which may be mounted directly on the primary disc. For many types of decorative work, it is often convenient to mount the workpiece on a smaller disc, known as the secondary disc, which can be positioned and locked more or less anywhere along a known reference diameter of the primary disc, via a slot in the latter, and a bolt through both discs.

▲ The finished clock face

> **"You can position and lock the router on the guide rods to cut a circle, or part-circle, of any desired diameter in the workpiece"**

The secondary disc has a number of equally spaced holes around its outer edge, which can be engaged by a pin mounted in a stop-block. Thus it is possible to position the centre of the secondary disc at a known fixed distance, offset, from the centre of the primary disc – and to rotate and lock it in a number of fixed angular positions relative to the reference diameter of the primary disc. This allows a variety of decorative scalloping operations to be performed on the workpiece, as we shall see.

Possibilities

The range of possibilities is further improved by means of a series of equally

> **"With the pivot-frame thus locked on the primary disc, it is possible to cut straight lines of predetermined length, simply by sliding the router on the guide rods"**

spaced holes around the primary disc itself. These can be made to engage with a pin dropped through an existing hole in one of the two pivot bars on the pivot-frame.

This is the simpler method – a far better one, comprising a spring-loaded plunger engaging with horizontal holes around the primary disc, *see Photo 2*, can be achieved. With the pivot-frame thus locked on the primary disc, it is possible to cut straight lines of predetermined length, simply by sliding the router on the guide rods – the length of cut being determined by two pairs of locknuts on the pivot-frame adjuster.

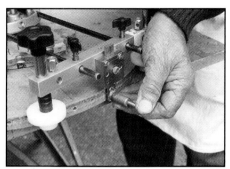

Photo 2 A spring-loaded plunger engages with holes in the primary disc

Clock face

The clock face is made from two basic sheets, the scalloped inlaid top, and the circular base plate. Although there is no particular difficulty in making the whole thing as a single item, it is much easier to sand and finish two items separately and join them afterwards – rather than attempting to deal with the complex junction area between the two, particularly if a high-gloss finish is required.

Because of the complexity of the top face, I recommend that the measurements given for this part are carefully adhered to. The diameter of the base plate may be varied a little to suit individual choice but the thickness of the two will be

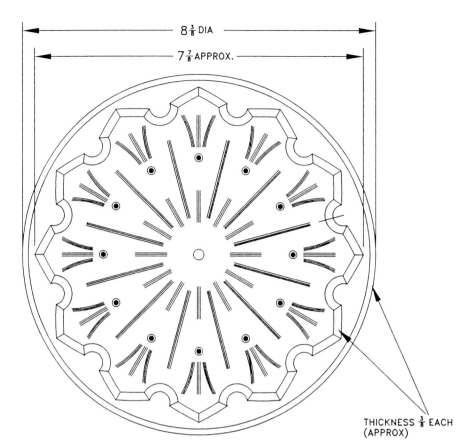

Fig 3 – all dimensions in inches

largely determined by that of the clock movement chosen.

I didn't want the overall assembly to be unduly thick, as this gives it a rather heavy appearance – and I found it better to use three hidden spacers to stand it off the wall a little.

The base

The base is a simple flat disc with a small cove machined on its top outer edge, *see Photo 4*. From a large single piece of timber, this is easily made with the pivot-frame in its beam trammel mode, using a 6mm (¼in) diameter hole in the centre as a pivot point.

The segmented construction allowed me to leave a rather large hole in the centre, to save timber, and, as a result, the work was carried out with the pivot-frame in its standard mini-pivot mode, *see Fig 1* – but, with the workpiece mounted in the dead centre of the primary disc with a sacrificial sheet of hardboard beneath it to prevent cutter damage to the latter.

Location

Initial location was done by eye, and hot-melt glue fillets used to hold the workpiece down on its outer edge – thus enabling a truly circular opening to be cut in the centre, which was then removed.

A scrap of MDF with a 6mm (¼in) hole in the centre was then machined to fit the hole in the workpiece exactly, thus allowing the latter to be relocated at dead centre, and held down via a clamping disc, using the central bolt. The outer diameter and cove were then machined directly on the pivot-frame.

Scalloped top

The real meat of the job lies in the scalloped top and the inlays. The maximum diameter, *see Fig 3*, serves only to determine the approximate size of the blank, since the final dimensions will be

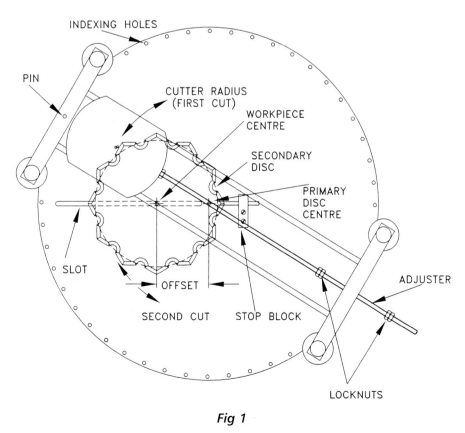

Fig 1

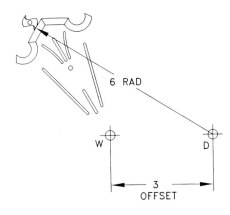

6 RAD

W   D

3
OFFSET

Fig 5 – all dimensions in inches

"Tiny cutters are not particularly good at clearing their own shavings, especially in a stopped channel, and are thus easily broken"

determined by the decorative cuts.

To begin with, it is necessary to use a large primary disc, in order to accommodate the given offsets. The router in the photographs is the old Elu MOF96E – the pivot-frame was originally designed around this particular router model – and is used with the long, 500mm, rods. The primary disc was made 490mm (19in) diameter – the maximum possible for this rod length.

Outer scallops

The outer scallops are machined, in 30° angular steps. For each angular setting of the 12-station secondary disc, it is possible to machine two opposing sections of the workpiece, *see Fig 5*. The diagram shows the detailed radius and offset requirements of this particular cut, showing one of the two possible cuts in its actual position relative to the reference axis of the primary disc. The letters W and D refer to the centre points of the workpiece and primary disc respectively.

All outer profiling is carried out with a 6.3mm (¼in) diameter straight cutter. The semi-circular incisions are made in a similar way, *see Fig 6*. Both decorative profiles can be cut with a cove cutter if preferred – a suggested figure being 16mm (⅝in) diameter as, with a cutter of this size, the only operation necessary is a cutter change, with the radius and offset values unaltered.

All the work may be carried out on a roughly circular workpiece blank but, in the interests of sparing the cutter and obtaining the best possible finish, I find it better to

"The real meat of the job lies in the scalloped top and the inlays"

scrollsaw the true scalloped profile slightly oversize to begin with, leaving only about 3mm (⅛in) to be removed by the cutter.

The problem of providing the initial profile is dealt with fairly easily by replacing the cutter with a marker made of a length of pencil lead in a metal rod – but beware, the lead is easily broken with this arrangement. I would recommend using this method if you are unfamiliar with pivot-frame offset operations, as it provides a degree of practice, and ensures that mistakes are not made when machining.

Curved inlay

The curved inlay channels are machined in the same way, *see Fig 7*, using a 1.5mm (¹⁄₁₆in) diameter cutter. It is necessary to limit the arc of travel of the pivot-frame, so that the cut stops at the two end points. Use

scraps of timber cramped either to the primary disc or the main worktop, so that they impede one of the nylon shoes at the appropriate point. But, for this reason, it is also necessary to machine all the left hand arcs at one setting, change the position of the stops, and then machine the remainder.

It is not a good idea to machine the inlay channels deeper than about 3mm (⅛in). Tiny cutters are not particularly good at clearing their own shavings, especially in a stopped channel, and are thus easily broken. Even a channel of the depth suggested is best machined in about three passes. Although it

▲ Photo 4 The face and base disc both have scalloped edges

is possible to make silly mistakes at any time, those involving inlays can place the cutter at risk as well as the workpiece – in particular, forgetting to lock all necessary adjustments before cutting and, perhaps worst of all, forgetting to retract the cutter before swinging the work round to the next angular station – this guarantees to break the cutter!

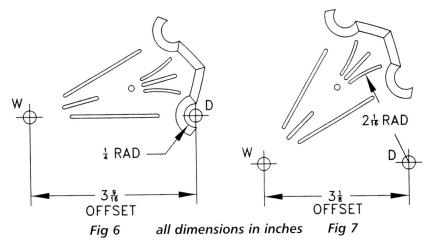

W   D   ¼ RAD   3 9/16 OFFSET   *Fig 6*   2 1/16 RAD   W   D   3 1/8 OFFSET   *Fig 7*

all dimensions in inches

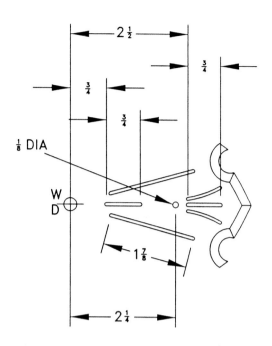

Fig 8 – all dimensions in inches

▲ Photo 9 Machining the channels for the inlays

Remaining inlays

The remaining inlays are machined with the aid of the indexing holes cut in the primary disc. Twenty-four equally-spaced holes are required in the disc, since, although each set of lines requires only 12 stations, there is a 15° angular offset between each set – my set-up actually has 48.

The workpiece is mounted at the dead centre of the primary disc for this operation and, whilst the secondary disc provides a satisfactory mount which may be locked in one position, its own indexing facilities are not really required in this case. Length of cut is pre-set with two pairs of locknuts on the pivot-frame adjuster, *see Fig 8*, giving all the necessary dimensions. *Photo 9* shows one of the channels being machined.

Firm control of lateral travel is required since, as mentioned earlier, it is easy to break tiny cutters. *Photo 10* shows my own preferred method, where the adjuster rod is being pulled along the slot, against thumb pressure on the pivot bar. *Photo 11* shows the completed piece.

▼ *Photo 10 Thumb pressure on the pivot bar gives firm control*

"The problem of providing the initial profile is dealt with fairly easily by replacing the cutter with a marker made of a length of pencil lead in a metal rod"

▲ *Photo 11 The face with all the inlay grooves routed*

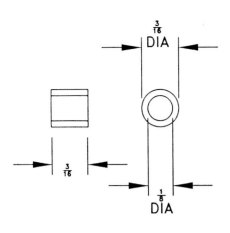

Fig 12 – all dimensions in inches

▲ Photo 13 The inner part in the two colour inlay is glued to a bolt ready for machining

Cylinders

Fig 8 shows the positions of the twelve holes. The easy option is simply to fill these with black plugs but, at the expense of a little extra work, it is possible to make them look better, *see Fig 12*.

Cut a number of short cylinders, bored with a central hole, which are in turn filled with another cylinder of contrasting timber. Despite their fragility, it is possible to machine them on the pivot-frame. *Photo 13* shows the completion of the delicate inner piece, which is machined by super-gluing a small scrap of timber to a suitable bolt, and setting the pivot-frame to a very small radius.

Inlays

The inlays are made up of a sandwich of white-black-white veneers, the outer layers being sycamore. It is possible to use ebony or blackwood for the centre layer, but these have an annoying tendency to leach or bleed their colour into the adjacent white layers during finishing, producing a rather muddy result. I prefer to use sycamore for all three, and to blacken the centre veneer by drawing it repeatedly across a hotplate, until it acquires the necessary colour – it does not need to be made dead black, wetting it will simulate the application of the finish, which will darken it.

It will be necessary to thin the veneers a little before gluing them together. I have a router jig to do this, but it can be done by careful sanding. The centre layer must be thinned before blackening, since it is too fragile for this operation afterwards.

▲ Photo 14 Glue-up the contrasting straight inlays on a flat surface

Straight inlays

The straight inlays are easily laid up with the aid of super-glue on a flat surface, with a polythene sheet beneath them to avoid unwanted adhesion, *see Photo 14*. The curved layers are similarly treated, but over a suitably curved former – they cannot be bent to shape after the sandwich has been glued.

The inner rods for the circular inlays are blackened in the same way, by rolling them backwards and forwards over a metal sheet laid on the hotplate. It is unlikely that they will be truly circular after this operation, but the discrepancy is minor and not noticeable. What does matter however, is that the blackening process will give rise to about a 15% reduction in diameter, and this must be allowed for when initially machining – some experimenting is necessary!

The inlays are cut to length and the ends rounded to match the cutter curvature with a little light sanding. Adhesion is best carried out with super-glue dropped into the bottom of the channels, or holes, with fine wire, and the inlay pressed in immediately – it should stand a little proud of the surface, *see Photo 15*. On no account should white glue be used, since this may cause swelling and jamming during assembly.

"The inlays are made up of a sandwich of white-black-white veneers, the outer layers being sycamore"

"Although it is possible to make silly mistakes at any time, those involving inlays can place the cutter at risk as well as the workpiece"

▲ Photo 15 Glue in the inlays using Superglue

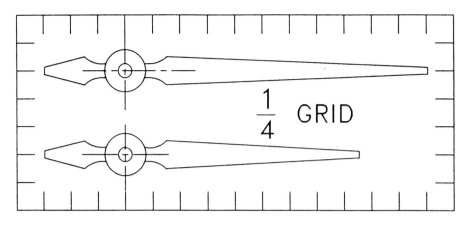

Fig 17 – dimension in inches

After assembly

After assembly, the protruding inlays are sanded down to the surface of the workpiece. Knifing or chiselling is best avoided, since this may cause a split in the inlay, and if this runs below the workpiece surface, it will produce a blemish almost impossible to correct.

Fitting together

Fitting of the clock movement is a relatively simple exercise, *see Photo 16*. The method illustrated is a further use of the pivot-frame, but any system which constrains the path of the cutter, and allows the placement of end-stops to limit lateral travel, is fine. For what it is worth, I tend to avoid producing templates for one-off jobs, as the time spent is often better employed directly on the workpiece.

The two halves may be simply glued together with white glue after finishing which, in my case, was with several coats of Rustin's clear plastic, rubbed down between each, and finally burnished to a high gloss.

The hands may be bought, usually from the same supplier as the movement, but I made my own in 0.79mm (½in) sheet brass, *see Fig 17*. Only basic dimensions can be given, since pivot holes will depend upon the clock movement used. ●

Clock movement and hand suppliers:
Craft Supplies, *tel: freephone 0800 146417*

"Knifing or chiselling is best avoided, since this may cause a split in the inlay"

Use a photocopier to enlarge drawings to required size or, for a full-size set, please send an A4 sae to: The Router (Clock Face), GMC Publications Ltd, 166 High Street, Lewes, East Sussex BN7 1XU

Photo 16 The clock movement is cut-in, also using the pivot frame

Armed against argument

MAKER

Bob Curran

No more rows about TV versus reading lights for **Bob Curran**, who makes a height-adjustable two-arm lamp

THIS universal lamp provides light that is perfect for both telly watching and for reading, so ending those disagreements which arise when partners seek separate amusements in the same room.

This is a fairly complex piece to make and I make no bones about assuming a certain amount of routing knowledge being required to complete some of the processes.

Some of the techniques I suggest are specific to my workshop equipment and I am sure that you will have other ways of achieving the same task. I hope that, like myself, all who attempt this project will enjoy the challenges it presents.

Before starting to machine any wood it is necessary to do some preliminary research. First, in order to establish the diameter of the wooden shade covers, the shades and bulb holders must be chosen. Screwed cable-entry bulb holders and screwed flanged back plates must also be selected prior to construction.

I assembled all the components of these bought-in parts to establish the depth of the recess in the shade covers, *see fig 1*.

"To make the bending jigs I used kitchen worktop offcuts, cutting a recess in the jig to accommodate a tap wrench"

Arms and legs
The arms and legs have severe curves in them so I decided to make them up from laminated strips.

Select two pieces of straight-grained oak (*Quercus sp*) boards, see cutting and materials

"Two bar clamps under the jig prevent it from breaking in two"

The design of the top fixing on shades varies. The depth of the recess for the bulb holder must be established to suit lampshade

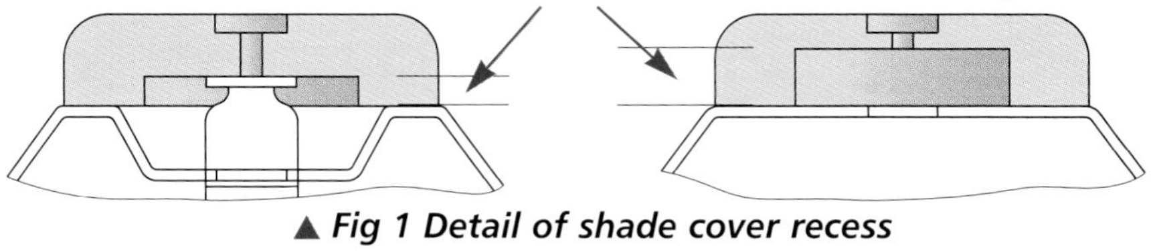

▲ *Fig 1 Detail of shade cover recess*

◀ *A lamp that helps to keep domestic peace*

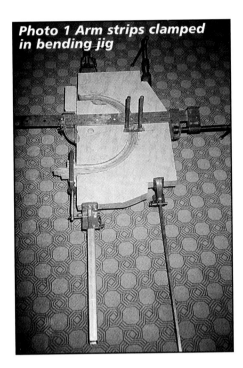

Cutting materials list

Item	Quantity	Dimensions
Arm	2off ex. 20off strips	2.5 x 20 x 550mm
Leg	4off ex. 32off strips	2.5 x 25 x 400mm
Table	1off	20 x 340 x 340mm
Disc	2off	20 x 180 x 180mm
Foot	4off	50 x 70 x 70mm
Shade cover	2off	25 x 110 x 110mm
Base	1off	50 x 150 x 150mm
Post top	1off	30 x 30 x 450mm
Post middle	1off	40 x 44 x 655mm
Post bottom	1off	40 x 44 x 340mm
Clamp bodies	2off ex. 4off	25 x 40 x 106mm
Clamp handles	2off	20 x 20 x 55mm
Clamp boss	2off ex. 1off	25 dia. x 50mm
Arm clamping screws	2off	5 dia. x 50 coach
Bolts, plated		
Bulb holder	2off	Brass, screwed
cable entry, earthed type		
Back plates	2off	Brass, screwed
cable entry		
Cable, 5 amp, twin-&-earth	6m	
Junction box	1off	5amp

Due to the precise nature of this project all dimensions are given in the metric sizes that the author specified.
For clarity, guards have been removed while taking photographs.

list, and plane one to 20mm thick and one to 25mm thick. To allow for inter-strip movement as the bending takes place, the strip lengths given are greater than required.

With a circular saw, cut off another 3mm strip, then plane the sawn edge of the boards as the starting point to cut off another 3mm strip. Repeat the planing and cutting until all the strips are produced, plus a few spares, then plane them finally to 2.5mm thick.

To make the bending jigs I used kitchen worktop offcuts, *see photos 1 and 2 and figs 2 and 3*, cutting a recess in the jig to accommodate a tap wrench clamp.

To glue the arms, apply glue evenly to the strips, but not between the sixth and seventh strips. This is so that the wire groove can be routed on the outside face of the inner curve prior to the two parts being glued up.

Apply the tap wrench clamp 250mm from one end of the stack of strips and place the whole lot in the jig. The strips are then bent by clamping up, *see photo 1*. Two sash cramps under the jig prevent it from breaking in two.

Leave to dry overnight, remove the assembly from the jig, separate the two pieces and repeat the process for the other arm.

Form the cable groove in the outer edge of the inner pieces by using a table-mounted router equipped with a clamped-on high fence.

Apply glue, return both parts of the arm to the jig, and reclamp.

With the glue still wet, push a spare piece of electric cable through the arm to ensure that no glue is blocking the groove. Repeat the process for the other arm.

When dry, clean up and sand the assembled arms.

The legs are produced in an almost identical way although this time, after applying glue to the leg strips, clamp them at one end before bending. Apply the second clamp when bending is complete. When the glue is dry repeat the process on all four legs.

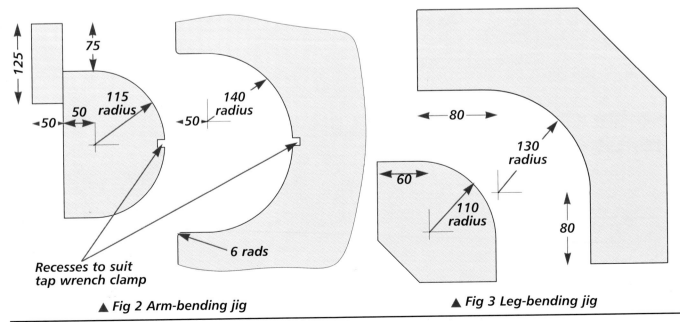

Recesses to suit tap wrench clamp

▲ Fig 2 Arm-bending jig

▲ Fig 3 Leg-bending jig

Routing operations

My router table consists of a piece of MDF suspended between the arms of the auxiliary table supports on my table saw. This enables me to pin or screw such things as jigs and fences to it, which would not be possible with a metal table.

Photo 3 The router in its home-made table and an overhead guide

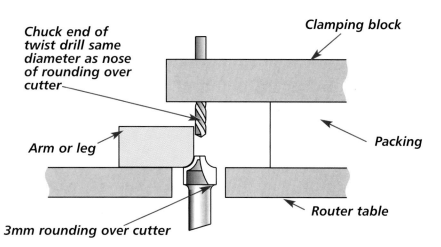

▲ Fig 4 Router set-up for arm and leg corner rounding

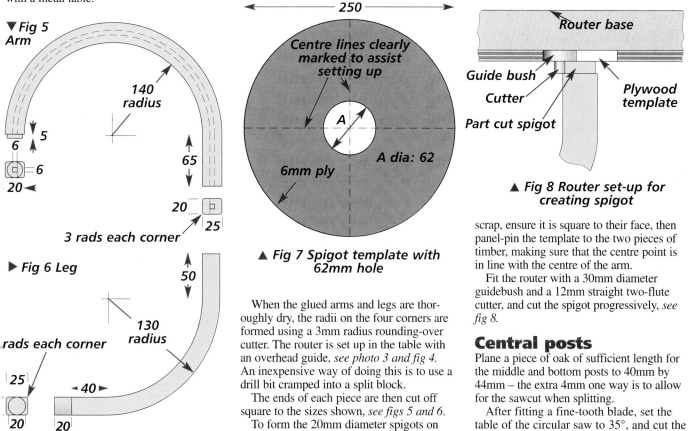

▼ Fig 5 Arm

140 radius

5
6
6
20
65
20
25

3 rads each corner

▶ Fig 6 Leg

50
130 radius

rads each corner

25
20
20
40

▲ Fig 7 Spigot template with 62mm hole

250

Centre lines clearly marked to assist setting up

A

6mm ply

A dia: 62

Router base

Guide bush
Cutter
Part cut spigot

Plywood template

▲ Fig 8 Router set-up for creating spigot

When the glued arms and legs are thoroughly dry, the radii on the four corners are formed using a 3mm radius rounding-over cutter. The router is set up in the table with an overhead guide, *see photo 3 and fig 4*. An inexpensive way of doing this is to use a drill bit cramped into a split block.

The ends of each piece are then cut off square to the sizes shown, *see figs 5 and 6*.

To form the 20mm diameter spigots on one end of each arm and leg, the template, *see fig 7*, is cut from 6mm plywood. Clamp an arm in the vice, between two pieces of

scrap, ensure it is square to their face, then panel-pin the template to the two pieces of timber, making sure that the centre point is in line with the centre of the arm.

Fit the router with a 30mm diameter guidebush and a 12mm straight two-flute cutter, and cut the spigot progressively, *see fig 8*.

Central posts

Plane a piece of oak of sufficient length for the middle and bottom posts to 40mm by 44mm – the extra 4mm one way is to allow for the sawcut when splitting.

After fitting a fine-tooth blade, set the table of the circular saw to 35°, and cut the piece in half along its length, through the centre of the 40mm thickness, *see figs 9 and 10*.

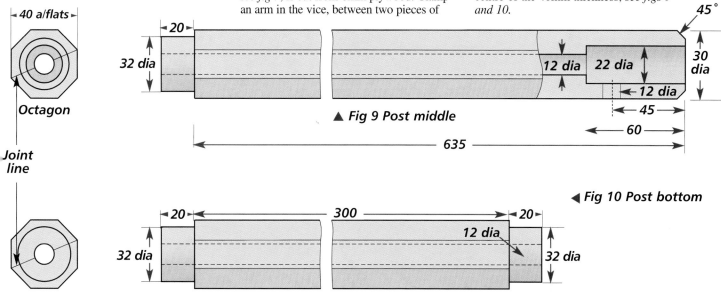

40 a/flats

Octagon

Joint line

20
32 dia

12 dia
22 dia
45°
30 dia
12 dia
45
60

▲ Fig 9 Post middle

635

◀ Fig 10 Post bottom

20
32 dia
300
12 dia
20
32 dia

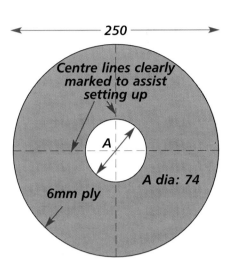

250

Centre lines clearly
marked to assist
setting up

A

A dia: 74

6mm ply

▲ Fig 11 Spigot template with
74mm hole

Photo 4
A template
and guide-
bush are
used to cut
the spigots
on the
ends of the
arms, legs
and posts

Photo 5 The spigots need to
be routed progressively

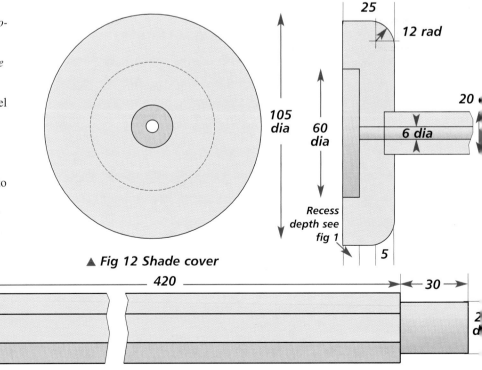

Photo 6 The middle post hole is drilled on a lathe

Using the router set up in its table and fitted with a 12mm diameter cove cutter, rout a semi-circular groove in the centre of the sawn faces. The two pieces are then glued together – again it is a good idea to place a piece of cable in the recess to stop excess glue from fouling.

When the work is dry, reset the saw table to 45°, cut off the corners and plane the piece to a 40mm across-the-flats octagon.

Cut the middle and bottom parts of the post to length so the joints that fit into the table and upper post can be created.

Using the template, see fig 11, machine the spigots on the ends of the posts in the same way as for the arms and legs, see photos 4 and 5.

Using a lathe, the 22mm diameter hole in the end of the middle post is drilled, see photo 6. Before drilling, I plugged the 12mm diameter hole, created by routing the wire recess, with a short piece of dowel to steady the point of my flat drill. The stump of the dowel is knocked out when the hole reaches the required depth. The 45° chamfer is then formed on each face on the top of the post to soften the edge.

The post top that the lamp arms clamp to is planed to a 30mm across-the-flats octagon and mounted between centres in the lathe. The 22mm diameter spigot and semi-spherical end are then turned, see fig 13.

Shades, base, table

Next, turn the shade covers, see figs 12 and 1. I mounted the band-sawn blanks on a small lathe face plate and turned the outside to a finish. The 20mm diameter spigot hole is achieved with a drill mounted in the tail-stock chuck. With a 12mm diameter cutter mounted in the router, the recess on the

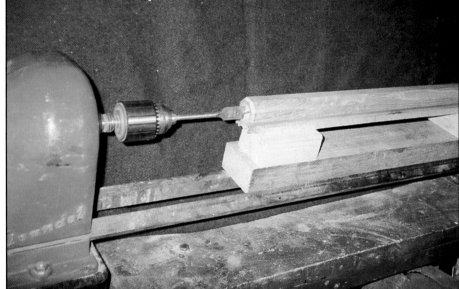

25

12 rad

105
dia

60
dia

6 dia

20

Recess
depth see
fig 1

5

▲ Fig 12 Shade cover

30 a/flats

Octagon

420

30

2
d

▲ Fig 13 Post top

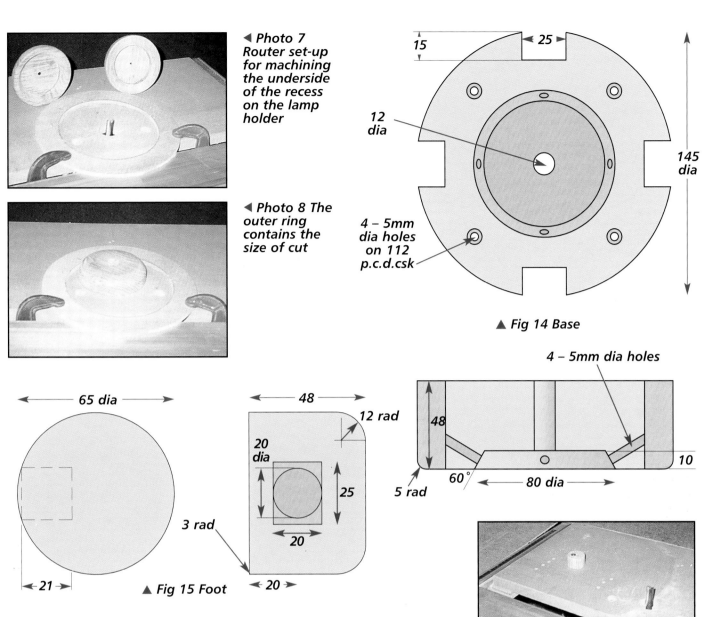

◀ Photo 7 Router set-up for machining the underside of the recess on the lamp holder

◀ Photo 8 The outer ring contains the size of cut

15 ◀ 25 ▶

12 dia

4 – 5mm dia holes on 112 p.c.d.csk

145 dia

▲ Fig 14 Base

65 dia

21

▲ Fig 15 Foot

48

12 rad

20 dia

25

3 rad

20

20

4 – 5mm dia holes

48

60°

5 rad

80 dia

10

▲ Photo 9 A boss with an off-centre screw is attached to the router table

▲ Photo 10 The disc is placed on the boss and its outside routed

underside is machined out in progressively deeper cuts, *see photos 7 and 8*. The diameter of the hole in the plywood jig is 153mm.

The base is a basic cylinder, and turning it is a straightforward operation, *see fig 14*. The four leg slots are hand-cut to suit each leg. The holes for the leg-retaining screws are then drilled.

Next the four feet are turned, *see fig 15*. The 20mm diameter holes drilled for the ends of the legs and, finally, the four flats for the ends of the legs are created by hand.

The three blanks for the table top and two discs are bandsawn to a diameter a couple of millimetres larger than the sizes shown, *see figs 16 & 17*, and the 32mm diameter holes for the post spigots are then drilled in their centres.

To set up the router table for machining these large round components, *see photos 9 and 10*, make a wooden 32mm diameter boss and drill the hole for a fixing screw 5mm off centre to give it a cam effect. Screw the boss to the table with its minor

axis toward the cutter and place the disc on the spigot.

Rout the edge of the disc, rotating it past the cutter. After a complete circle is routed, twist the boss to move the disc nearer the cutter, and machine again, repeating the process until the correct diameter is achieved.

When the outside diameters are to size, the 12mm diameter straight cutter is replaced with a 25.4mm diameter cove cutter, and the profiled edge is machined.

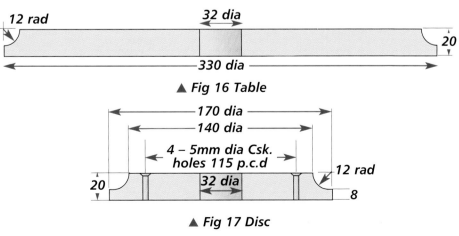

12 rad

32 dia

330 dia

20

▲ Fig 16 Table

170 dia

140 dia

4 – 5mm dia Csk. holes 115 p.c.d

32 dia

12 rad

20

8

▲ Fig 17 Disc

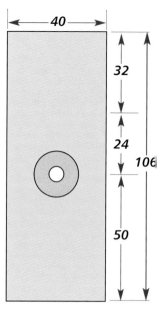

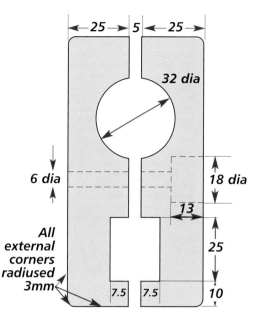

▲ Fig 18 Clamp bodies

Clamp and finish

The clamp parts complete the project. A 5mm by 50mm coach bolt passes through the clamp body *see fig 18*, and its head sits inside the 18mm recess. This is then covered with the small cap, *see fig 19*.

Metal nuts are pressed into the 10mm diameter holes in the clamp handles, *see fig 20*, and secured with epoxy resin. The longer small hole is to take the end of the coach bolt.

▲ Fig 19 Clamp boss
◄ Fig 20 Clamp handles

The completed parts, *see photo 11*, are finish-sanded and then given three coats of satin polyurethane, the final one being cloth-applied with a few drops of oil mixed in.

To wire up, twin-and-earth 5amp cable is used, one piece from each lamp holder being threaded through each arm, allowing sufficient length to accommodate the maximum movement of the arms, before passing them into the post and down to the base.

A junction box is screwed to the underside of the base where these two cables are joined to a single piece of cable.

This cable, into which a torpedo switch is wired about half a metre from the box, runs to the plug and socket. Please have the wiring checked or carried out by a qualified electrician.

Then sit down and enjoy the effect of this unusual lamp. ●

▶ Photo 11 Completed parts ready for assembly

◄ Fig 21 Exploded view of lamp

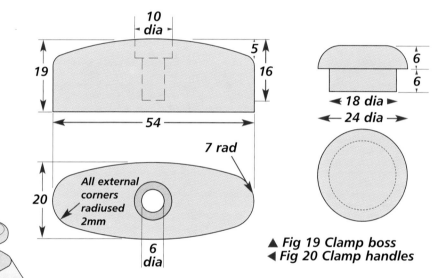

Under the thumb

Ian Hall engineers an element of mystique into a display cabinet

ILLUSTRATIONS BY IAN HALL

MAKER
Ian Hall

MY wife was becoming increasingly frustrated at the way her collection of porcelain thimbles, ornaments and Chinese vases was growing a fur coat while displayed on open shelving and pigeon-holes, so I made this small wall-mounted cabinet with shallow shelves and glass front.

Design, planning

The cabinet is in pearwood (*Pyrus communis*), and the construction is essentially an exercise in mitring, with three frames mounted concentrically one on top of the other.

The front assembly lifts up, clear of the rear wall-mounted frame, leaving the bottom of the middle frame behind, so exposing the shelves.

This movement is achieved by guide slots machined respectively into the middle and rear wall frame. When the unit is closed the front comes down to rest, locating on the false-bottomed middle section as though it is part of the complete frame.

This not only provides some mystery to its opening, but false tenons add to the secret. There are of course no hinges or catches. The spacing and type of shelving are completely optional, with my example showing lipped glass shelves.

The lipping was an incredibly laborious task and I admit that the next cabinet would have plain polished edged glass epoxy-glued into the side slots.

The plan, *see diagram*, gives the cross-section of all the frame parts to the exact sizes of the cabinet and, because the cross-section of each frame is the same all round, they can be routed in one length to the finished section before mitring.

Note that the front glazed and middle frames are finished completely before starting the rear wall frame. This cabinet is about as big as it can go due to the weight of the glass.

Front frame

Start by making the front glazed and middle frames. Their side lengths are all the same, which means fewer set-ups when it comes to mitring. I prefer through, loose tenons for jointing – 6mm (¼in) cut from scrap pieces of the pear.

▲ *A thimble display cabinet*

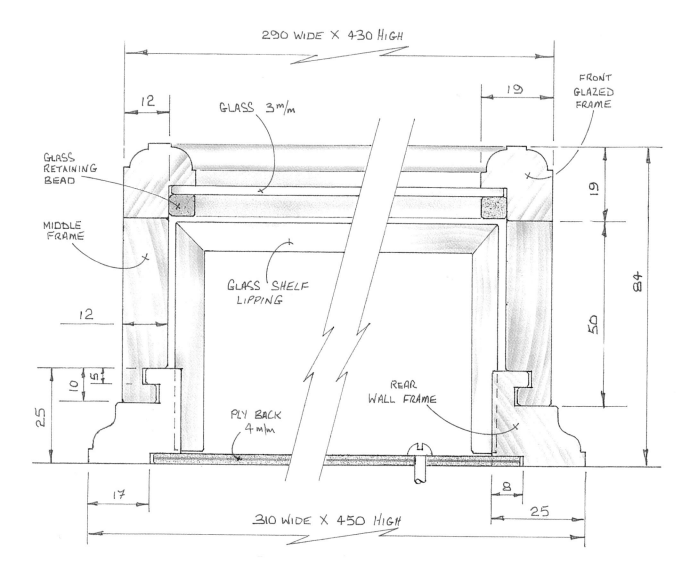

290 WIDE X 430 HIGH

FRONT GLAZED FRAME

12

GLASS 3m/m

19

GLASS RETAINING BEAD

MIDDLE FRAME

GLASS SHELF LIPPING

REAR WALL FRAME

PLY BACK 4m/m

12

19

84

50

25

10

5

17

8

25

310 WIDE X 450 HIGH

The front frame consists of a rebate to take the glass – a beading is added later to secure the glass – and a moulding formed by two passes of the same cutter. I used a 22mm diameter ovolo cutter.

The stock can be machined using either a table-mounted router, a side-fence or bearing-guided cutter. However, with these small sections a router table has the added advantage of requiring no jig-making.

Failing that, machine the moulding onto a wider piece of wood, then cut off in strips.

The slots for the loose tenons in the end frame were cut using a 6mm double-fluted cutter with the end of the workpiece against the router table fence and a stop to set the position of the cut.

After machining, clean up the round end of the slots with a chisel and, to avoid breakout, cut the mitres before the slots.

The loose tenons can be cut out on a saw from 6mm (¼in) planed stock and tried for fit before final gluing up. This front frame is butt-glued to the middle frame later on.

▲ *Full-scale horizontal section*
◀ *Details of the bottom of the rear wall frame*
▶ *Cutaway of the front frame and bottom of the rear wall frame*

Middle frame

The middle frame is jointed in the same way, with one edge housing the first groove which forms the sliding joint.

The 5mm guide slot and tongue in the middle frame are not compulsory dimensions. You may choose to alter the size slightly to suit your own cutter availability. In reality, the 5mm slot should be slightly oversize and the tongue in the rear frame slightly undersize to prevent the sliding action from binding.

Once the middle frame is glued you are committed to size, but the rear wall frame can be adjusted to fit it.

Cut to length and mitre the ends of the sides. Machine the 6mm slots for joints and decide at this time whether

to add the false tenons as they are better
fitted and flushed off now rather than
after assembly.

Then produce tenons to fit snugly and
long-grain across the slots.

Decide which is to be the top and
bottom of the middle frame, then put the
bottom piece to one side until ready for

final fitting. After a few dry runs to ensure
an accurate fit, assemble the middle frame.

Glue the front frame together, then,
with its face down, carefully place the
three-sided middle frame on its back,
without glue, while the glue in the
mitres dries. When dry, butt-glue the
two frames together.

Rear wall frame

A close look at the scale plan shows very
little clearance for the shelves – totally self-
inflicted on my part. I suggest that the
25mm (1in) wide moulding is 'beefed' up
to, say, 30mm (1¹³⁄₆₄in) in width to give
more room for manoeuvre, especially if
you've chosen to fit solid glass shelves.

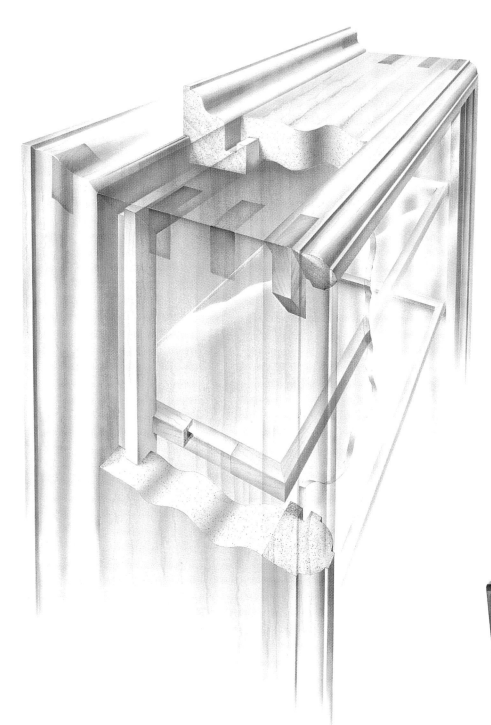

◀Cutaway of the middle frame on the top of the cabinet
▼The front of the cabinet slides up to gain access to the inside

Assembly

Plan to run the loose tenon slots through the middle of the outer moulding, then glue up the assembly. When dry, begin the routing around the outside, using a piece of scrap wood of the same section as the frame to set up the router.

To make the frame more solid for routing, the ply back should be glued and pinned.

Rough off excess material and then nibble away around the frame until it will fit the front assembly.

Allow the front assembly to slide fully home, then glue the false bottom of the middle section to the rear wall frame. A little sanding here will avoid binding and cause a snug meeting with the mitres.

Finishing

I gave my case several coats of Danish oil over several days, and finally waxed it to ensure a smooth action in the guides.

Finally, the front glass is pinned in with a bead. ●

Plan your outer ogee moulding – I gave mine gave a 10mm step down to the middle frame.

For several reasons, it is easier to rout the ogee moulding and the other sliding groove once this frame is glued up: firstly, because the 6mm loose tenons pass through the middle of the outer moulding, the router cutter will automatically flush them off as they are created; secondly, you would be very lucky to get a satisfactory fit of the guide slot in the middle frame if it were machined before mitring; thirdly, the frame is easily hand-held when applied to your router.

First, rout only the rebate for the plywood back. Then, having decided the side lengths of the frame components, cut and mitre them.

The spacing for the shelves must be decided, and the appropriate width slots run into inner edges of the vertical frames; alternatively the shelf spacing can be given total flexibility by inserting slots every 20mm ($^{25}\!/_{32}$in), and the shelves positioned as need be.

Tooling up

■ 5 and 6mm double-flute straight cutters
■ 10mm double-flute or rebate cutter
■ 22mm diameter ovolo cutter
■ 19mm diameter Roman ogee cutter

MAKER

Anthony Bailey

Stoke the fire

Anthony Bailey warms up his router making a pine fireplace surround

A FIREPLACE is a perfect focus for a room, however existing fireplaces often lack something i.e. an impressive surround to show it off to best effect. Here is a design that will transform your living room and put the heart back into it!

I have used softwood, because it is cheap and can be purchased ready prepared. The sizes shown on the drawings are only for guidance because each household's requirements are different.

Fluting the uprights

Cut the uprights to length and mark out the fluted sections allowing for the plinth blocks beneath. Likewise mark where the reeded strips will go (*see drawing*) – the space remaining should be sufficient to take the roundel design. Mark this out on each stile ensuring it is centred.

Using a corebox bit of 16mm diameter rout the flutes in the uprights on the router table, having first put pencil marks on its

reverse side and on a subfence attached to the table's fence. This means you can 'drop on' and start and stop the cuts accurately. Move the fence between cuts to get the right spacing – use a trial piece each time to check that it looks OK. Remember that the workpiece can be reversed to rout the flutes at the other side of the column, rather than laboriously resetting the fence for every single fluting operation. Getting an even result takes a bit of care and will start with accurate marking out.

> "Getting an even result takes a bit of care and will start with accurate marking out"

▲ *The flutes are routed by lining up pencil marks and lowering the workpiece onto the cutter*

Roundels

The roundels need to be machined at the top of each column. This is done freehand using a thin sub-base of MDF screwed onto the router's baseplate using whatever threaded holes are provided. Fit a panel bead cutter which gives a suitable roundover effect for the centre 'boss'. The outer rings are cut with a 6mm straight bit – measure the distances needed to give the correct radius for each operation (several are needed to get the final effect). ▶

> "Here is a design that will transform your living room and put the heart back into it!"

▲ *The pine fire surround ready to fit*

▲ *A sub-baseplate is made to machine the roundels*

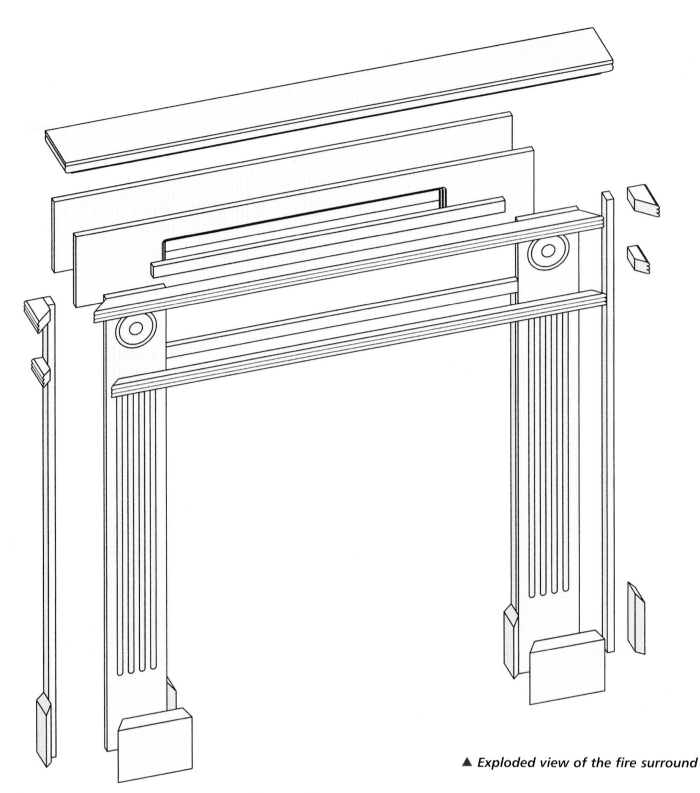

▲ *Exploded view of the fire surround*

Mark these positions on the sub-base and drill at each position ready to take a small piece of studding. Make the drill hole slightly smaller than the studding – say 4.5mm for a 5mm diameter stud. Thread the studding into the first hole, then drill. Use a test piece and make a circular pass to create the roundel effect. Move the studding to the next hole, change to the straight bit and carry on machining until the whole thing is complete. The outer ring is created with the panel bead cutter again with a new stud hole so it is offset to the outside of the slot. Rout this with the straight bit. The result is that with care only the outer edge of the slot will get rounded over. Check that it looks OK, then do it for real on the columns.

Crosspiece

Cut the crosspiece to length allowing for it to go most of the way behind the columns which it will be glued and screwed onto. Mark out the recess in the middle that will have a moulded edge. I was originally going to make an MDF template to suit this shape and use it with a bearing guided 'classical' face mould cutter. However I had just finished making my new spindle moulder sized router table so I was keen to try it out, rather than using a template. I cut the recess out by 'dropping on' and running the workpiece against the fence, the ends are routed using the protractor to guide it. Remember that several passes are needed to cut right through to full depth. As I didn't have a template suitable for a classical cut-

ter with a top bearing, I chose the good old 9.5mm ovolo instead as its bottom bearing will run around the recess. Glue the panel behind the recess and fix with panel pins.

Glue the crosspiece or fascia behind the columns and screw from behind ensuring all is square.

Columns, plinths and mouldings

Next cut some spare 25mm (1in) or 19mm (¾in) thick wood or MDF into strips and glue and pin these behind the columns down the full length of each side to make them look deeper than they really are. Do the same with the underneath edge of the crosspiece, these pieces need to sit against the wall once the mantle shelf is fitted.

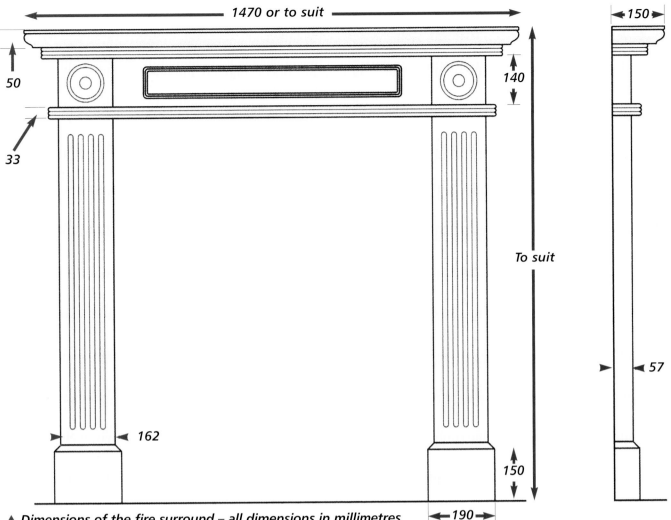

▲ *Dimensions of the fire surround – all dimensions in millimetres*

1470 or to suit

50

33

140

To suit

150

162

150

190

57

panel cutter was slightly narrower than the prepared stock so I used the point on a marking gauge to whittle off the slight overhang on the edges before sanding.

Mitre and fit all the reeding making sure it runs level all the way round. To make up the gap where the crosspiece sits back from the face of the uprights cut strips of stock the same thickness as the columns and the same width as the mouldings. The top moulding is set flush with the top edge of the surround, ready for the mantelshelf to sit on. I used PVA and panel pins for fixing them on, followed by a rub of filler in each hole.

Mantelshelf

The last major job is machining the solid mantelshelf (ex 50mm [2in] stock). I was going to use a very large ogee cutter belonging to a friend, it would

▲ *A straight cutter is plunged through the workpiece to create the cut-out in the crosspiece*

To make the plinths, rout a 45° angle on the front of a wide board using a bevel cutter. Cut pieces to length and mitre the corners around the base of the columns. Glue and pin them in position.

The projecting reeded edges are created next using 33mm (1⁵⁄₁₆in) wide (finished size) stock and a reeding or ogee panel cutter. If the cutter you have isn't wide enough, reverse the workpiece and rout it twice to give a double width of reeding. Note how the upper section of reeding projects further than the lower one to give better proportion, this is easily achieved by using thicker wood. I found the ogee

"I was going to use a very large ogee cutter belonging to a friend, it would have looked nice – but he'd gone on holiday!"

▲ *The cut-out is then moulded on the front making sure fingers are kept well clear*

▲ On the reeding use the point of a marking gauge to cut off the waste left by the cutter

▲ The ends of the mantelshelf are tricky to rout, an extension to the table will help

have looked nice – but he'd gone on holiday! After a bit of head scratching I settled on a trusty Wealden Grecian ogee which is normally intended for skirtings.

Routing the cuts across the grain is the most difficult as you need to support a quite substantial piece of wood, without it tilting, while running it carefully over the cutter. A through fence helps as does some kind of extension fixed to the side of the table.

I screwed a scrap piece on the back at the edge of the mantelshelf to stop the breakout that would normally occur. Rout the left edge, then the front edge, lastly the right edge. To get the right depth quite a few passes are needed so as not to overload the router or cutter. The overhang may be a little uneven on the underside, this can be cleaned up with a sharp chisel, then sanded. Invert the mantelshelf and glue and

screw it to the surround, using strips of softwood if necessary.

Finishing

Whether your fire is ever lit or not, it is wise to seal the reverse of the pine as well as varnishing or applying sanding sealer to the front as it will be more stable. Use mirror plates fixed to both sides of the columns to attach it to the wall, ensure that the wall fixing screws are set close to the columns so that as the pine shrinks with room heat, the screws will slide in the mirror plate holes. Use a metal primer on the mirror plates and then use emulsion paint the same colour as the walls to disguise them.

The result is a grandiose fireplace that will impress all your friends. ●

Tooling up

■ Wealden Cutters used
■ Two-flute, bearing-guided rounding over cutter

■ Point round cutter – for reeding
■ Core box cutter
■ Bearing-guided sunken profile cutter

▼ The cutters used

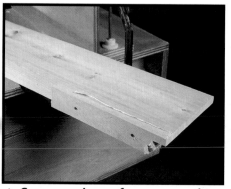

▲ Screw a piece of scrap wood to the back of the mantelshelf to stop breakout

MAKER

Anthony Bailey

Anthony Bailey

Anthony Bailey with
some hot tips on making
radiator covers

Radiating style

R ADIATOR covers – once the
province of posh clubs for the
rich and famous – are now play-
ing a stylish part in many home
decoration schemes. They are relatively
simple to make with router and cutters –
and can represent a profitable little side-
line for professionals.

Design factors

They must be wide enough to allow for the
radiator valves to be operated, and not so
shallow that, should a hot radiator move
away from the wall, the grille panel would
be pushed off.

The proportions of the cover can be
changed to suit, perhaps by increasing its
height or length or by upping the number
of grille panels from two to three. Where
possible, all radiator covers in one room
should be set at the same height.

I build mine from 18mm (¾in) thick
MDF because it is cheap and stable
enough to cope with heat variations.
Making from solid wood isn't a realistic
option as it tends to move a lot with
extreme changes of heat, although the
same effect can be obtained by using
veneered MDF with thin solid wood
mouldings around the edges.

On a sheet of paper, and to a convenient
scale, sketch out the board size 2440 by
1220mm (8 by 4ft). Draw on this the
width and number of strips of all the components required in order to devise the
most economical cutting plan.

Carcass construction

A portable circular saw and a straight-edge
does for ripping everything slightly oversize. Then plane all the edges smooth with
a router, *see photo*.

Cross-cut components to length with the
exception of the plinth and grille frame
parts, which are dealt with later, *see photo*.

▲ *The sheet of MDF is trimmed to size and edges
cleaned up with a router*

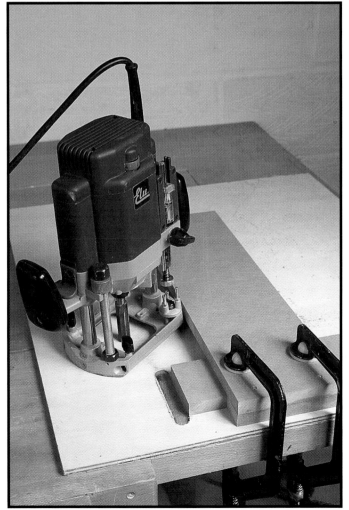

▲ *Small components need a jig to aid with dimen-
sioning*

"I machined the top's edge moulding with the router inverted in a table, but free-hand routing it is also possible"

A short strip jointed onto the base of the carcass ends creates a step to accommodate the grille frame, *see photo*. This is achieved with a biscuit-slotting cutter used in the router. For safety's sake, leave these strips long for the slotting process, cutting them to length afterwards, *see photo*.

Note that each slot is marked in the centre and on either side. This enables the router to be moved along so that a slot long enough to accept a '20' biscuit can be created.

Glue these pieces in place and leave to dry.

I machined the top's edge moulding with the router inverted in a table, but free-hand routing it is also possible.

First, produce the major curve by routing a largish roundover, then use a 6mm diameter roundover cutter to rout the top again, but on the other side, *see photo*. Applying two curved mouldings on opposite sides of a board will inevitably leave a slight point where the workpiece runs against the fence, but this can be sanded out.

The long edge is easy to machine, but take care to give maximum support to the work-piece when routing the ends with the fence gap set small, *see photo*. A steady hand while pushing the board past the cutter will help, with any slight deviation in cut being sanded smooth afterwards.

Next, use a square to mark the underside of the top, so providing lines for the outside of the end panels, *see photo*. Joint these with biscuits and mark them accordingly.

Cramping on an 'L' jig, *see photo*, allows the router to slot the underside of the top while the more conventional approach is used for the slots in the panel ends. Dry-fit the

"Cramping on an 'L' jig allows the router to slot the underside of the top while the more conventional approach is used for the slots in the panel ends"

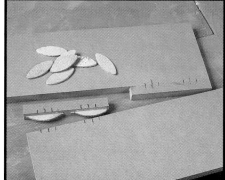

▲ Short blocks are biscuit-jointed to the base of the carcass ends to accommodate the grille panel

▲ For safety, rout the biscuit slots before cutting the blocks short, feeding in at the far end first to avoid kick-back

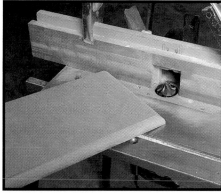

▲ The moulding on the top is formed using a large roundover cutter followed by a smaller one on the other side

▲ Use a false fence with a small gap to support the workpiece when routing the ends

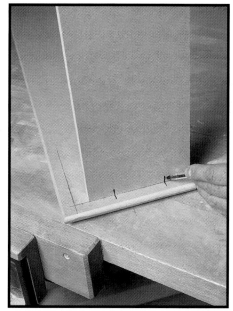

▲ Mark the positions for the biscuit-jointing slots

▲ A right-angle jig aids biscuit slotting inside the ends of the top

Grille choices

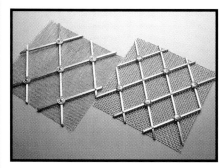

Grille possibilities vary from expensive brass in diamond, rosette and mesh patterns, to cheap punched hardboard obtainable in a number of patterns ready for painting. Any of these can be fitted in place, using panel pins or a tiny wooden fillet, after finishing the cover.

   If using a paint finish, ensure the cover and any hardboard grilling is primed. Denib between coats before applying a top coat of gloss, satin or decorative paint effect.

▶ The grille fitted into the panel

▲ Various grille types can be used according to budget, brass from the most expensive brass diamond, rosette and mesh pattern, punched through polished brass to punched hardboard

Tooling up
- Biscuit-slotting cutter
- Straight-fluted cutter
- Large roundover cutter
- 6mm diameter roundover cutter
- Moulding cutter – any classical profile, for example Grecian ogee or Victorian torus
- 45° V-cutter
- Profile and scribe cutter set
- Bearing-guided rebating cutter
- Titan 3mm roundover bit

---

ends and measure across at the top to arrive at the correct width for mitring the plinth.

Plinth
The plinth moulding can be a Grecian ogee, *see photo*, a Victorian torus or any suitable classical profile. Run the moulding on enough stock to go round the cover, allowing extra for mitres and mistakes.

The mitres can be cut either with a mitre saw or, preferably, with a router fitted with a large 45° V-cutter, the work being run against a T-square fence.

Trim the ends of the long piece of plinth so that the distance between the internal mitre corners is the same as the previously taken measurement, *see photo*.

Now butt-glue this plinth piece in place,

cramp and check the cover for square by measuring the diagonals from corner to corner, *see photo*.

Cut two small blocks of MDF, apply glue to two of their faces and rub them into the internal corners between the plinth and the end panels. The blocks will back up and strengthen the plinth's butt-glue joints, *see photo*.

▲ The plinth looks good with a Grecian ogee moulding

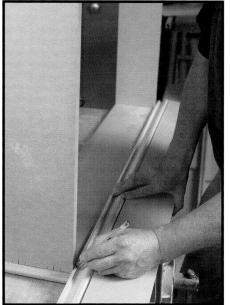

▲ Carefully mark the inside edges of the mitres

▲ Firmly clamp the plinth in place until the glue is dry

▲ Glue blocks inside the cover to help hold the plinth in place

▲ Front and side elevations

▲ The grille panel frame is easily made using a profile and scribe cutter set

▲ Mark out the ventilation slots top and bottom of the panel

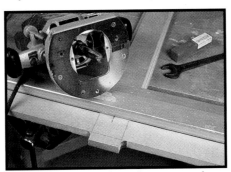
▲ Using a straight-edge, rout the ventilation slots

▲ Make sure the grille panel is square when cramping-up

▲ Add a decorative moulding with a 3mm roundover cutter

"Fit it tightly before planing top and bottom to enable the panel to be removed for access to the radiator taps"

Cut and mitre two short lengths of plinth, one for the right-hand end and one for the left. Glue them in place, butting them up tight to the existing mitres, and cramp up.

The top edge of the long plinth must be backed up with a 30mm (1⅛in) strip of MDF, glued in place to strengthen the narrow edge of the moulding. Ensure no gap shows below the grille panel.

Glue the top in place. When dry, fill and sand any gaps or blemishes.

Grille panels

The grille panel is the same width as the cover, and the height is the distance between the top of the plinth and the underside of the top. Fit it tightly before planing top and bottom to enable the panel to be removed for access to the radiator taps.

The side rails, top rail and intermediate uprights – muntins – are 75mm (3in) wide. Perspective effect means the bottom rail looks better if it is about 15mm (⅝in) wider than the other components.

Use a profile and scribe cutter set to make the frame, adding 19mm (¾in) to the length of the top rails, bottom rails and muntins to allow for their scribe cut, *see photo*.

Leave the stiles overlength for trimming after assembly.

Set up the router table with the cutter in scribe mode, and rout the ends of the rails, and the muntins supporting them, with a push-block or protractor fence. Leave a minimal gap in the fence to prevent workpieces pulling into the cutter as they come off the bearing.

Reset the router with the cutter in profile mode, then, by taking test cuts on offcuts, check that the profile lines up correctly – without a step – with the scribe-cuts on the rail ends when the joint is assembled.

As components must be turned over for this operation, play safe by marking the face to be profiled.

Mark the centre positions of the muntins on the rails and place a matching mark in the centre of the ends of each muntin.

Pre-sand all the moulded edges, glue and cramp all the frame parts together, measuring from corner to corner to ensure squareness, *see photo*.

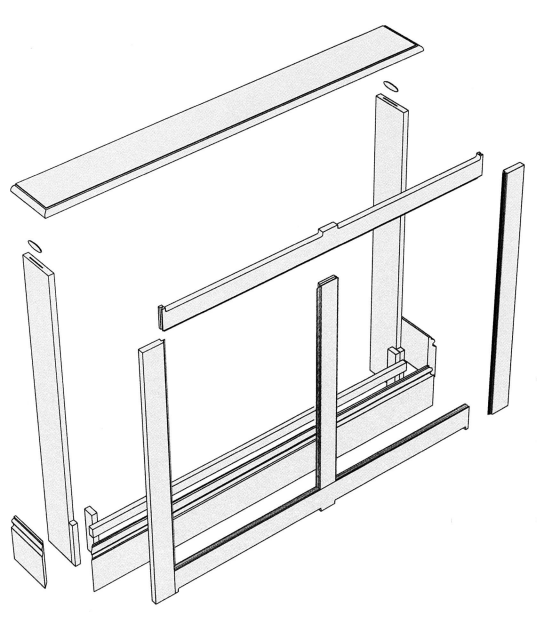

◀ *Exploded drawing of a radiator cover*

▼ *Radiator covers look good with a painted finish*

"The radiator cover must be scribed along its back edge to fit as closely as possible around the skirting board and accommo-date any unevenness in the walls"

Once dry, trim the panel frame to a loose fit in the carcass, using a straight cutter in the router and running it along a straight-edge, starting with the two long edges. When sized correctly, sand all round.

Use a bearing-guided rebating cutter to achieve a 10mm rebate for the grille.

For the ventilation slots at the top and bottom of the panel, *see photo*, mark them out and then make successive stopped cuts so they line up with the muntins, *see photo*. A 3mm Titan roundover bit, set to make a slight step, achieves a nice moulded finish to the slots, *see photo*.

Finishing, fitting

The radiator cover must be scribed along its back edge to fit as closely as possible around the skirting board and accommodate any unevenness in the walls. Place a level on its front and tilt the cover accordingly.

Open a pair of compasses up to the widest gap between the wall and the cover and mark a line all round the cover, keeping the point of the compasses in contact with the wall and skirting.

Jigsaw along this line to achieve a tight fit that may still need a bit of tweaking.

Fix the cover with screws and masonry plugs, first checking for pipes and wiring. ●

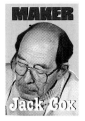

MAKER

Jack Cox

Jack Cox
goes full circle engineering a hand mirror

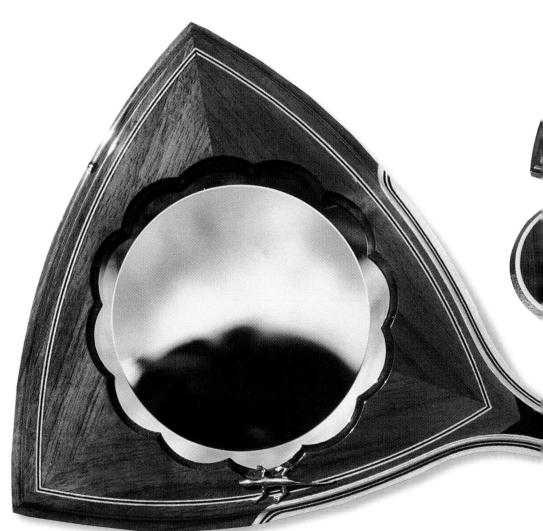

Arcs and pa

THE HAND mirror illustrated is basically an exercise in trammel routing, with all machining in the form of full circles or arcs.

For the larger arcs any form of trammel device, comprising a beam or bar with a pivot at one end and the router at the other, will do.

For smaller arcs my own preference is for the Trend Pivot Frame jig — my invention — because its ski system construction means the only contact between the router and the workpiece is at the cutter.

The jig
The jig comprises a pair of light-alloy 'pivot bars' which can be fitted to the router guide rods. Each bar carries a pair of nylon 'shoes' which rotate about a fairly large

circular 'primary disc'.

The 'ride height' of the router above the workpiece can be adjusted in steps using spacing collars between the pivot bars and shoes.

The router may be slid along the guide rods and locked in position to cut a circle of any radius within the limits of the disc. Small adjustments can be made with a large hand-operated nut on the central length of 'studding'.

The workpiece is mounted on a small 'secondary disc', with 24 equally-spaced holes bored around the periphery. Any of these holes can engage with a metal stop-rod mounted in a block, fitted to the primary disc.

The workpiece may be offset from the centre of the primary disc by a predeter-

mined amount, and rotated on the secondary disc in a series of angular steps, to machine 'scallops'.

The secondary disc is fitted with a central bolt which runs in a slot in the primary disc.

A similar arrangement is possible with the jig in its beam trammel configuration.

Mirror body
Assemble and glue three identical segments, cut and sanded on a disc sander, *see fig 1b*. I used well-seasoned American black walnut (*Juglans nigra*) for its stability.

The beam trammel set-up consists of a wood block with a hole bored through, into which is fitted a length of metal studding that also screws into a tapped hole in one of the pivot bars. Remove the shoe fitments from the pivot bar and level the

router base with spacers at the other end.

Attach the mirror body assembly dead centre onto the secondary disc, with fillets of hot-melt glue on the sides and also on the underside where it overhangs the disc, *see photo 1*.

Set the inner cut of a straight-fluted cutter to a radius of 200mm (8in) and offset the centre of the disc from the pivot point by 136mm (5⅜in), *see fig 2*, then set the stop rod. Cut off the extreme points of the blank to enable it to pass sufficiently close to the pivot point.

The first flank is routed, then the remaining two are cut by rotating the disc through 120°.

Next mount the assembly onto the Pivot Frame and rout circular rebates for the mirror backing and the mirror itself, *see photo 2*.

◀ *All the parts ready to assemble*

Photo 1 *Machine the edges of the mirror body with the Pivot Frame jig set up as a beam trammel*

Photo 2 *The Pivot Frame jig has white nylon shoes riding on a primary disc — ideal for routing the rebate in the back of the mirror body*

◀ *The completed hand mirror*

rquetry

Copper lizard

The home-made copper lizard covers a new piece of timber I had made a mess of fitting while seeking to rectify a black mark on one of the inner scallops.

Rout the channels for the inlays by setting the inner cut of a $1/16$ in diameter cutter to a 193mm ($7 \frac{5}{8}$ in) radius, avoiding over-run of the cutter at the joint lines. The slight radius left by the cutter is easily removed with a small chisel. The 3mm ($1/8$ in) deep channel is cut in three passes, *see photo 3*.

To rout the internal scallops a fixing plate must be made. Attach two small sheets of hardboard, with a central hole for the bolt, to the secondary disc, adding a small fillet of hot-melt glue to prevent unwanted rotation.

> "To machine the internal scallops a fixing plate must be made"

The top hardboard disc is machined right through in small concentric steps to provide an exact fit within the rebate of the workpiece. Fit it over the disc, registering it with the aid of the joint lines, and hold it with fillets of hot-melt glue.

The scallops may now be cut, *see fig 1*, using a straight cutter machined completely through the remaining thickness of the workpiece. Cut the coves in the same way, but with a cove cutter, after suitable radius adjustment. The indexing system is used on alternate peripheral holes to provide 12 scallops.

The handle
The handle is made from a single piece of timber, set up so that a pair of opposing arcs may be cut, producing the required shape, *see fig 2*.

Reproduce the relevant part of the drawing to size and stick it to the work with double-sided adhesive tape, *see photo 4*.

Adjust the radius and set it so that the inner cut traces the outline. To avoid contamination of the cutter by the tape adhesive, partially cut back the drawing with a craft knife before routing.

The ebony (*Diospyrus ebenum*) 'spacer' between the frame and the handle is rather difficult to produce accurately, since it must provide a good tight fit to both the frame and the handle, *see fig 3a*.

It is best made in two mirror-image halves machined as one, *see photo 5 and fig 3*.

The two half-profiles are glued one above the other to a piece of scrap timber and machined together, *see fig 3b*. They are then glued together, followed by assembly to the handle and the frame, *see figs 3c—f*.

Side laminations
Now make a template that allows a bearing-guided rebate cutter to machine the recesses

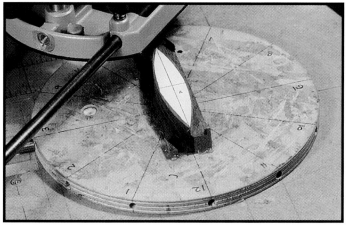

Photo 3 **Rout the channels for the inlays and the internal scallops**

Photo 4 **Stick the handle pattern to the work with double-sided adhesive tape**

at the sides of the frame; these carry the laminations, *see fig 2 and photo 6.*

The template need not cover all the actual handle. Small scraps of ebony left on the handle are bandsawn away, followed by a little sanding, to maintain a smooth profile, *see photo 7.*

If a cutter of the correct dimension isn't available cut a slightly deeper recess and add more laminations.

Laminate each sycamore (*Acer pseudoplatanus*) veneer strip in stages, starting at the junction of the frame and handle, and attach them with thin, free-running, fast-acting glue, *see photo 8.*

The black strips are not ebony or blackwood (*Acacia melanoxylon*), but are also sycamore, slowly and carefully blackened over a hot-plate. This prevents natural black dye from leaching into the white areas, but unfortunately makes them brittle, so needs careful handling.

The veneer will follow the curvature, except at the rather sharp bends midway along the frame where it may crack unless given a little initial help. Dampen the veneer and press it with a heated brass or light alloy rod about 13mm (¹/₂in) diameter into the curve of the workpiece, before applying adhesive — do not use steel rod as it may discolour the veneer.

Inlay

The inlaid strips, comprising three veneer layers each, are

"If a cutter of the correct dimension isn't available cut a slightly deeper recess and add more laminations"

Fig 1

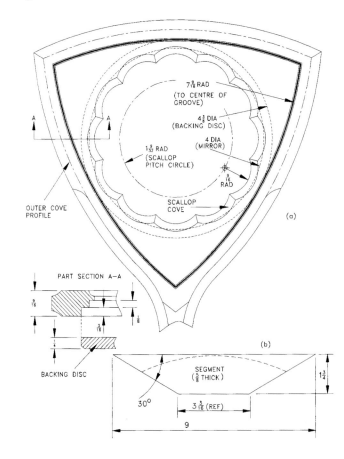

see fig 2 and photo 6.

Parquetry de

Bevel the edge of the backing disc and make it stand a little proud of the frame as a long-term 'hair-line' flush joint is difficult to achieve.

Cut the disc oversize before producing the curved parquetry profiles with a small adjustable beam trammel which has a point at one end and a veneer knife at the other.

The black sections are fragile, heat-blackened sycamore; the grain direction is most important, see fig 4b.

Firstly, the three main sections 'A', see fig 4a, are cut with accurate joints between them. They are treated as plain segments, ignoring the central design, and trimmed to a slightly oversize circle. They are taped at the joints, and also taped firmly to a cutting mat, using transparent plastic adhesive tape.

Extend the joint lines across the full diameter of the work with a pencil for reference when making the small straight cuts at the centre.

Draw the two refer-

Photo 5 *The ebony 'spacer' is best made in two mirror-image halves machined as one*

Photo 6 *Make a template for using a bearing-guided rebate cutter to machine the recesses at the sides of the lamination-carrying frame*

Photo 10 *The kit required for making the decorative back*

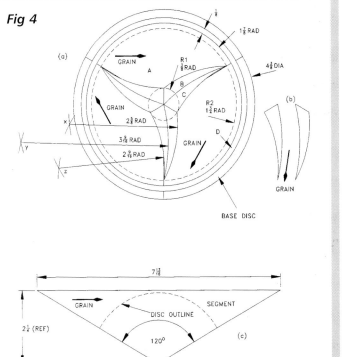

Fig 4

ence circles 'R1' and 'R2' onto the veneer with compasses. These circles are used, together with the three joint lines, to locate the ends of the arcs of the small segments 'B' and 'C'. From these points, arcs — see fig 4a for radii — are drawn on the cutting mat to locate the three centres 'X' , 'Y' and 'Z'.

Pencil lines can be made more visible by placing small pieces of transparent tape in appropriate areas and re-drawing over them.

Set the cutting trammel to the 'Z' radius and cut the arcs on the assembly; with the trammel at the same setting cut the inner edge of the three black segments.

Reset the trammel and repeat the process for the 'X' radius, cutting both the assembly and the outer edges of three white inlay pieces.

The cut-out centre section of the assembly is removed, one of the black pieces fitted against its corresponding arc and taped along the joint, see photo 10.

Transparent tape is also placed over the intended cutting line. With the trammel set to the 'Y' radius, the piece is now cut to size. The inner straight line is cut using a straight-edge.

Fit the white piece and cut its inner edge with the trammel still set on the 'Y' setting; repeat the procedure for the remaining two sets; cut the straight line and fit in place.

Trim the outer circle of the whole assembly with the trammel. With the same setting cut the inner diameter of the surrounding ring from a single piece of veneer; the outer diameter is carefully cut after resetting the trammel.

Fit to the main assembly with transparent tape.

The assembly is removed from the mat, turned over, and taped all over on the underside in two or three broad strips of brown plastic parcel tape. The transparent tape on the top side is now replaced with gummed paper tape, ensuring that all joints are covered.

The brown tape is removed from the underside and the veneer assembly stuck to the base disc with PVA glue.

The paper tape is damped and removed, and the entire disc sized, bevelled, sanded and finished to choice.

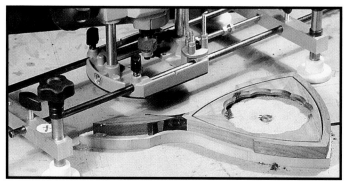

Photo 7 *Rout the mirror sides using the template*

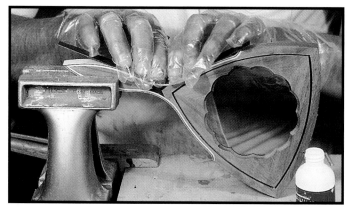

Photo 8 *Laminate each veneer strip in stages, starting at the junction of the frame and handle; attach them with thin, free-running fast-acting glue*

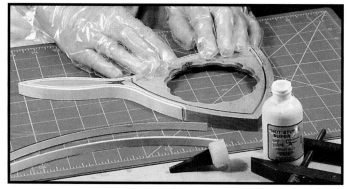

Photo 9 *Use a more viscous glue for the inlays*

Fig 2

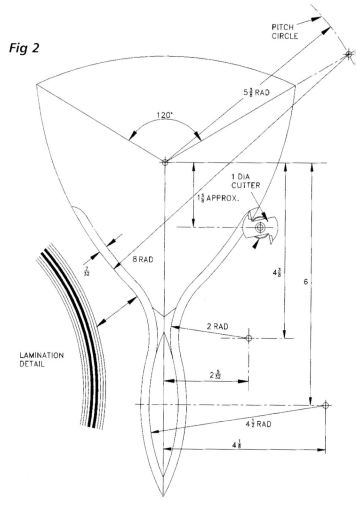

LAMINATION DETAIL

PITCH CIRCLE

$5\frac{3}{8}$ RAD

120°

1 DIA CUTTER

$1\frac{5}{8}$ APPROX.

8 RAD

$\frac{7}{32}$

$4\frac{3}{8}$

6

2 RAD

$2\frac{5}{32}$

$4\frac{1}{2}$ RAD

$4\frac{1}{8}$

Fig 3

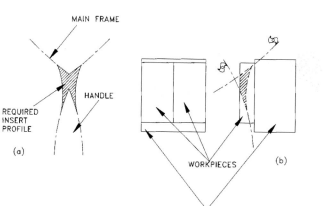

MAIN FRAME

HANDLE

REQUIRED INSERT PROFILE

(a)

WORKPIECES

SUPPORT BLOCK

(b)

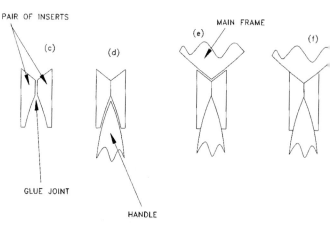

PAIR OF INSERTS

(c)

(d)

MAIN FRAME

(e)

(f)

GLUE JOINT

HANDLE

bent over an MDF former, made at the same time as the main frame, and glued with a more viscous grade of fast-acting glue.

They will retain sufficient curvature to enable them to be fitted into the grooves quite easily, *see photo 9*.

The inlays should stand proud of the channels before careful chiselling and sanding flush.

Finally, the workpiece is held down with a large ply disc and a central bolt, and the edges profiled back and front with a suitable bearing-guided cove cutter.

Backing disc

A backing disc, *see panel*, fits the rebate to hold the mirror in place and my parquetry design, *see fig 4a*, has a press-fit enabling the mirror to be removed and replaced if broken.

The basic disc is a three-segment construction, joined the same way and in the same timber as the frame itself, *see fig 4c*. ●

Use a photocopier to enlarge drawings to required size or, for a full-size set, please send an A4 sae to: *The Router* (Hand Mirror), GMC Publications Ltd, 166 High Street, Lewes, East Sussex BN7 1XU

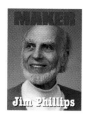
Jim Phillips

Trend founder **Jim Phillips** routs a little box from the solid

▼ *Trinket box complete with felt liner*

Boxercise class

SMALL boxes can be made in a variety of ways. Round and oval-shaped ones which involve no jointing skills might appear to be a doddle, but there are a few routing problems to be overcome if the box is to be exclusively router-made and look really professional.

When the router is set up to cut and shape small objects, it has to be maintained absolutely level as any tipping will be reflected in unevenness in the cut edges. Levelling devices can be bought to maintain the router square to the work, but my self-made ones will help those working to a small budget.

The production of this small mahogany (*Swietenia macrophylla*) trinket box is really a template exercise, with the router being used in the portable mode. Without doubt, readers will suggest other ways of making it, but I hope my method of construction will enthuse those interested in working with templates.

The floral design on the lid was hand-routed, using a series of Trend Carving

Templates, but the small rebate and sunk-edging bead were machined with the router mounted in a Craft router table.

> **"When the router is set up to cut and shape small objects, it has to be maintained absolutely level as any tipping will be reflected in unevenness in the cut edges"**

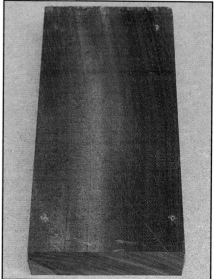

▲ *Photo 1 Secure the workpiece to a workboard*

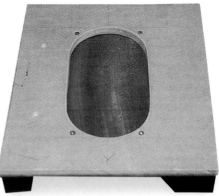

Photo 4 With the depth of the router set to no more than 2-3mm, increase the depth at each clockwise rotation around the template until down to 25mm is reached

◄▲ *Photo 2 and 2a Cut a generously sized template to use when cutting the inner rim of the box*

'Inside' template

First, secure the workpiece down to a workboard, *see photo 1*. If screwing down, do it in the waste area and countersink the screw heads.

Then rout a groove which will form the inside rim of the box. This procedure requires a template, *see photos 2 and 2a*, cut from 8mm ply with an aperture 16mm (⅝in) larger all round than the finished product.

Note the generous overall size of the template, which allows for the router base to ride over its surface, and avoid tipping during the routing operation. The template must be raised exactly level to the workpiece face, and four corner blocks are glued to its base for this purpose.

A level position is important because this avoids the router base catching on any high points during the operation.

With the template in position, fit an 8mm long-reach cutter into your router, together with a 40mm guidebush, *see photos 3 and 3a*.

◄▼ *Photo 3 and 3a With template in position, fit an 8mm long-reach cutter with a 40mm guidebush into your router*

First, run the router around with the template, *see photo 4*, to check for a smooth obstruction-free movement.

"Regularly suck the dust from the groove as some may have lodged there following each pass"

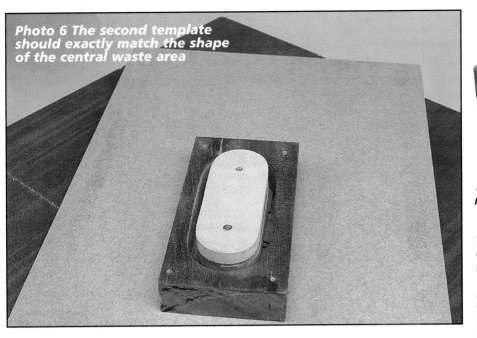

Photo 6 The second template should exactly match the shape of the central waste area

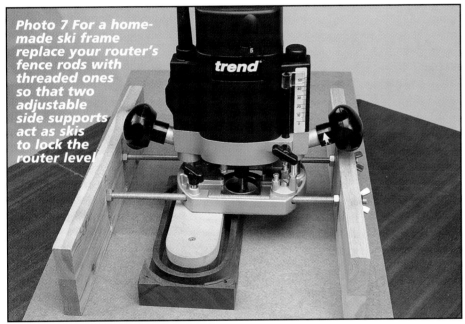

Photo 7 For a home-made ski frame replace your router's fence rods with threaded ones so that two adjustable side supports act as skis to lock the router level

Photo 8 With the outer rim cut, the waste surround can be removed

▲ *Photo 5 The central waste area remains in place to act as an anchor*

Now set the depth of your router to 2-3mm (⁵⁄₆₄ to ⅛in), switch on and feed clockwise around the template.

Increase the depth at each round to achieve 25mm (1in). This leaves a wall thickness of 7mm (⁵⁄₁₆in) on the base of the box. During this procedure, regularly suck the dust from the groove, as some may have lodged there following each pass.

Now remove the template, leaving the workpiece still secured to the work board, *see photo 5.* Note that the central waste area should still remain in place as this provides the 'anchor' for a new template for cutting the outer rim of the box.

"Depth is increased approximately 2mm at a time until the cutter is approaching the point of breakthrough"

'Outside' template

Cut a second template in 8mm ply or MDF. This template should exactly match the shape of the central waste area, and should be screwed down into it. Countersink the screw heads to ensure a smooth face, *see photo 6.*

To raise the router level with the template, a 'ski' frame is needed.

A useful innovation is to replace the standard fence rods of the router with threaded ones. This enables two adjustable side supports to act as skis, locking the router level with the template surface.

Trend's Pivot Frame Jig System offers a ski accessory.

Using the same cutter and guidebush, make a series of anti-clockwise sweeps around the template, *see photo 7.*

Depth is increased approximately 2mm at a time until the cutter is approaching the point of breakthrough. Then remove the waste area carefully.

With the outer rim cut, the waste surround can now be removed, *see photo 8.*

Photo 9 Remove the bulk of the interior with a 50mm Forstner bit

Photo 10 Finish cleaning out with a router ski frame set-up

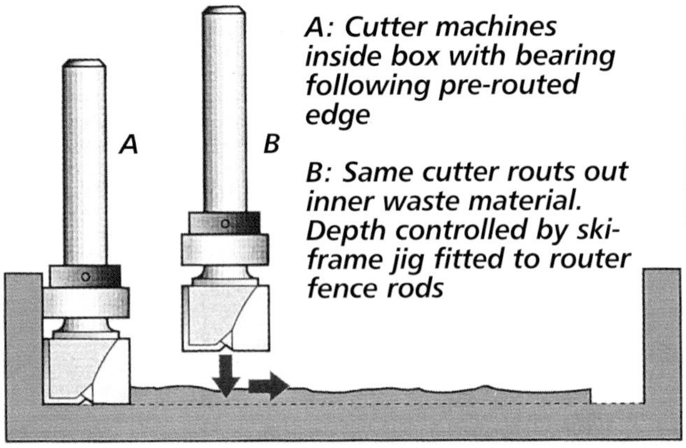

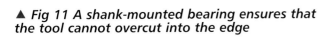

A: Cutter machines inside box with bearing following pre-routed edge

B: Same cutter routs out inner waste material. Depth controlled by ski-frame jig fitted to router fence rods

▲ **Fig 11** A shank-mounted bearing ensures that the tool cannot overcut into the edge

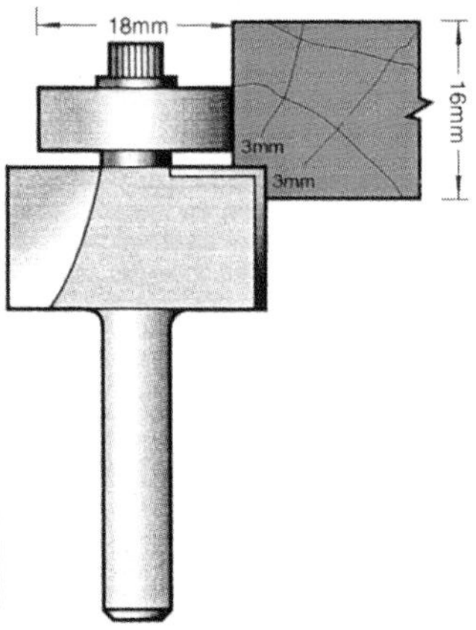

▲ **Fig 12a** Trend's 46/44 guided rebate cutter

▲ **Fig 12b** Trend's 8/20 guided bead cutter

Size of box

Outside dimensions:
178mm (7in) max

Inside dimensions:
162mm (6⅜in) max

Height of box, less lid:
32mm (1¼in)

Lid thickness:
16mm (⅝in)

Tooling up

All from Trend
■ *3/40L router*
■ *GB40 40mm guidebush*
■ *Ski accessory from the Pivot Frame Jig System – optional*
■ *46/91 16mm cutter*
■ *46/44 guided rebate cutter fitted with 18mm dia. bearing*
■ *8/20 guided beading cutter*
■ *Craft Table*
■ *Carving templates*

Plus
■ *50mm Forstner bit*

The bulk of the box interior can be removed with a 50mm Forstner bit, *see photo 9*, and the remainder routed out, *see photo 10 and fig 11.*

The base internal area is smoothed using a straight 16mm cutter with a guide-bearing of the same size mounted on its shank. The router is fed backwards and forwards to remove a millimetre or two at a time.

Finishing

The lid is cut in two operations on a Craft Table from solid 16mm material, *see photo 12 and figs 12a and 12b.*

First, using Trend's 46/44 cutter fitted with an 18mm diameter bearing, cut a small 3mm rebate. Then, using their 8/20 cutter, achieve an attractive finish by cutting a sunk bead edging.

To overcome the bland design, I used a series of templates from Trend's Carving Template range to achieve a floral pattern on the lid, *see photo 13.*

A felt liner completes the trinket box. ●

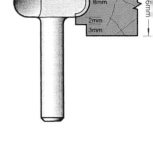

Photo 12 Finishing the lid

▲ **Photo 13** Using Trend carving templates for the lid

Boxes of tricks

Alan Goodsell temporarily deserts the Editor's chair to make a versatile piece of furniture

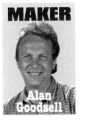

MAKER

Alan Goodsell

I originally created this piece of furniture for my new video, *The Router — a Beginner's Guide*. It is designed to be made using simple techniques, easy to obtain timber and fittings, a router and a 12-piece starter set of cutters.

The piece is an exercise in modularity: make one as a cabinet; make two to go either side of a bed; join the two with a top and you have a dressing table or desk.

The units can be made as all-drawer versions or with a door.

Materials
To avoid having to plane-up stock, mine is constructed from ready-made DIY store pine boards and fittings.

Although boards are available in various lengths and widths I decided to use 500mm-wide material for the carcass components, 200mm-wide for the drawer fronts and split in half for the skirting; the drawer boxes are made from 300mm-wide material ripped in half, with various widths for the rest, *see cutting list.*

Dimensioning
Cut all the components to size, making sure that all edges are square and true. The router is ideal for accurately dimension-ing stock. Using a housing or rebating technique, take the cut in stages, right through the wood — the only drawback to this method is the large width of cut.

Carcass
When creating the housings for the carcass floor, use a straight-edge as a fence for the router to run on, either a home-made version, or a bought one, *see picture.*

Install a straight-fluted cutter. As this type of wood is usually 18mm thick an 18mm cutter would be preferred; failing that, use one of a smaller diameter and rout the housing in two passes.

With the mains power to the router off, measure the distance from the edge of the baseplate to the nearest cutting edge of the cutter, then measure from the edge of the baseplate to the other side of the cutter. With my 12.7mm cutter the measurements were 66 and 78.5mm respectively — note them down for reference when positioning the fence.

With a pencil, mark the position of the top of the floor, *see marks 1*, at the front and back of both the carcass sides, then mark the thickness of the floor down from them, *see marks 2* — a scrap of the correct thickness timber is useful for this. The top

▲ *The bedside cabinet*

▲ *Measuring the distance from either side of the cutter to the edge of the baseplate*

▲ Mark 110mm up from the bottom of the carcass side

▲ Mark the thickness of the floor with scrap timber

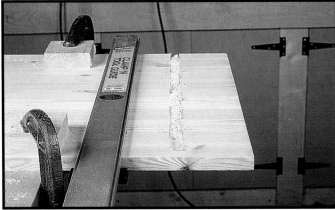

▲ Move the guide to line 2 and rout the housing to width

▲ Square-up the rounded ends with a chisel

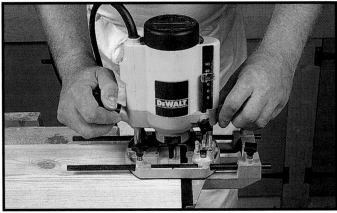

▲ Rout the rebate in small steps then square the corners

▲ Left- and right-hand carcass sides

of the floor is 110mm up from the carcass bottom; the 100mm-wide skirting then has something to butt against.

Mark the positions for the fence, position 1 at 66mm from mark 1, and position 2 at 78.5mm from mark 1.

At the end of the housing make a mark 20mm back from the front edge on each carcass side — this is the point where the housing will stop.

Set up the fence on position 1 then, after setting the depth of cut at 9mm, rout on the first part of the housing; stop at the 20mm mark. Repeat this on the other carcass side, but plunge in at the 20mm mark to ensure the cutter is rotating against the feed direction.

Follow this by fixing the fence at position 2 and rout the housing to the finished width. Clean out the round edges of

the stopped housing with a chisel.

Saw 20 by 9mm cut-outs on the front edges of the floor to allow it to sit flush with the front edge of the carcass.

The rebate for the back can now be cut. Attach the side fence to the router and set it to take a small cut at the same depth as the housing. To reduce the chance of the wood splintering, machine this small rebate

all the way along the back, inside edge of the carcass sides. Then increase the cut in stages until the rebate matches the thickness of the back, in this case 18mm.

Mark out for a small rebate to house the top rail on the top of the carcass. With the same set-up rout it carefully in stages, 15mm back from the front edge, 18mm wide and 70mm back from the front edge.

▲ *Using the cutter - to - baseplate measurements mark positions for the fence*

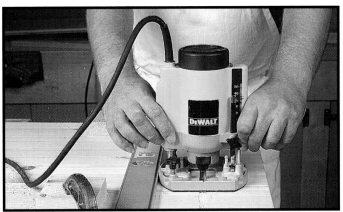

▲ *Attach guide to line 1 and rout the housing, starting 20mm from the edge*

▲ *Cut out the ends of the floor*

▲ *Mark the rebate for the top rail*

▲ *Simple to make mortice and tenon jigs — note the guide bush in the mortice jig*

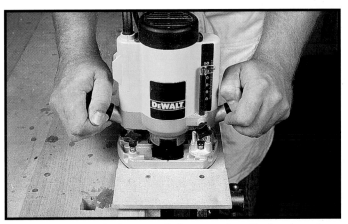

▲ *Clamp a workpiece and the mortice jig in the vice and rout to depth*

Again, rounded corners will need squaring with a chisel.

The 70mm wide top rail needs a 15 by 9mm cut-out on its front edges. Using a couple of sash cramps, glue and cramp the two carcass sides to the floor — modern glue is strong enough on its own to hold all firmly together.

Apply glue to the ends of the top rail, fit it into its housing then pin in place. Measure the diagonals of the carcass to check for square, then leave to dry.

Run a line of glue into the back rebates and pin the back in place to complete the carcass.

Tops, bottoms

The top is simply cut to length and an ogee moulding run on three sides — to stop breakout a block is clamped on the last across-grain edge to be moulded.

To locate it in place on the carcass, attach two battens to the underside; a few screws will fix it in place later.

This time the ogee moulding is run from the top edge, so cramp two pieces of skirting together to create a more stable platform for the router.

Cut mitres on the skirting and screw on the side pieces from inside the carcass. The front piece is glued in place — I have always found this to be

Tooling up

Trend 12-piece starter set Clamp and tool guide

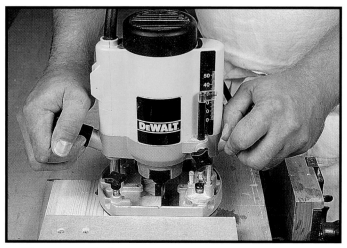

▲ The tenon jig is easy to use

▲ The tenon should be a snug fit in the mortice — see marks for stopped chamfer

▲ A stopped chamfer gives the door interest

▲ A look inside the cabinet shows how the runners and hinges are fitted

Goodsell's tips

⚠ Never handle a router cutter without first turning off the mains power to the router

⚠ Always wear the correct safety equipment

■ Use scrap pieces of wood for setting-up

■ When routing a moulding around a board, always machine the first cut across the grain to prevent splintering

■ Make sure the carcass and drawer box are square across the diagonals

Fittings and other materials

■ Pair of 350mm long roller runners
■ Pair of 110° cabinet hinges
■ Handle for drawer
■ Knob for door
■ Various length screws
■ 30mm oval nails
■ Wood glue

"The top is simply cut to length and an ogee moulding run on three sides"

strong enough, but small blocks can be screwed inside for extra strength.

Drawers

Bought-in metal roller runners solve many drawer-making problems; their use results in a drawer that will take a hefty load and still run freely.

To allow for the runners the drawer box has to be about 25mm narrower than the inside measurement of the carcass.

For a strong joint I used the easy to make housing and rebate type, created in a similar way to the housing in the carcass, but with a 6.3mm straight cutter.

Rout the housings in the

drawer sides with one pass of the cutter, the back of the cut being 18mm from the front. Then rout the rebates in the front and back, ensuring that the tongues fit snugly into their respective housings.

A 6.3mm wide by 9mm deep groove for the plywood drawer bottom is routed in the sides and front. Run it all the way along the sides; on the fronts, stop just short of the ends or else the groove will show. Cut off the bottom portion of the back at this point.

Glue and cramp the drawer box together and slide in the bottom. Square the box across the diagonals, then knock a few pins through the bottom into the

back to hold it in place.

The drawer front is cut to size then, using a bearing-guided ogee cutter, run the moulding around its edge — start with a cut across the grain.

Attach one part of the metal drawer runners to the drawer and the other to the carcass sides — the front of the drawer box should be flush with the carcass. Drill four holes in the front of the box and screw on the drawer front from inside.

If a unit with three drawers is being made, space them equally apart vertically.

Door

The door is made from the same thickness stock ripped to

65mm wide. The side rails are 600mm long and the top and bottom rails are a couple of millimetres under the width of the carcass minus twice the thickness of the door side rails plus the length of two 20mm tenons. The doors have to end up the same width as the 397mm drawer fronts.

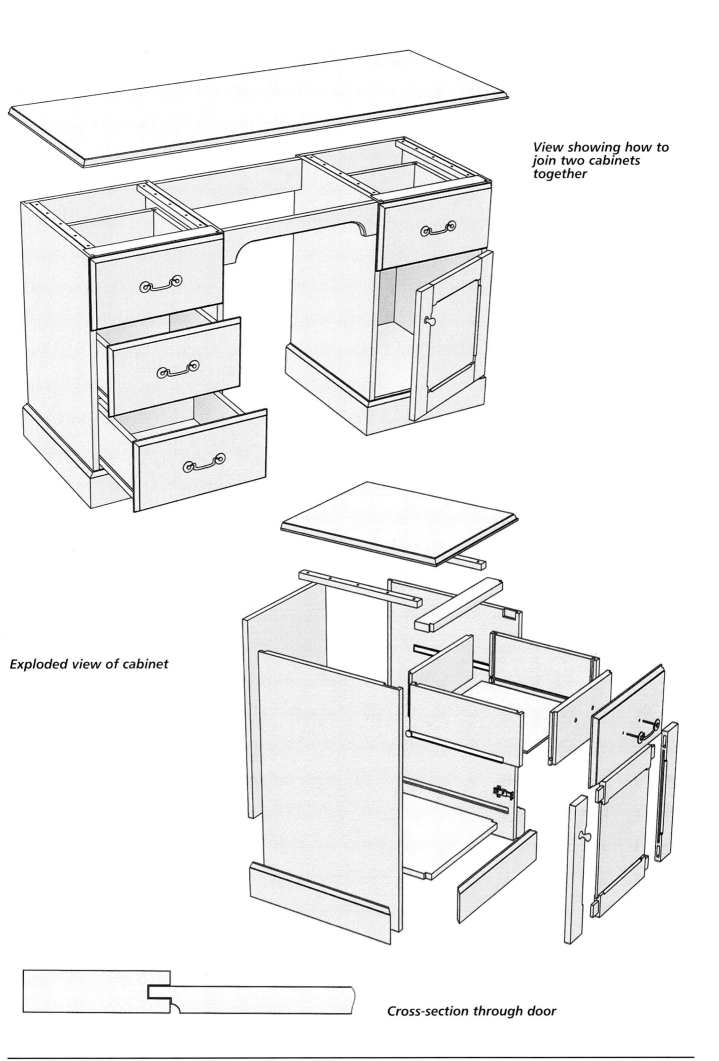

Exploded view of cabinet

Cross-section through door

▲ Screw the drawer front on from inside the drawer

▲ Fix two cabinets together to create a desk/dressing table

"To reduce the chance of the wood splintering, machine this small rebate all the way along the back, inside edge of the carcass sides"

▲ The same procedure is used to mould the top and drawer front

Using any preferred technique, mortice and tenon the door components, again using the 6.3mm straight cutter. The jigs shown are easy to make and use.

A 9mm deep groove for the panel must run centrally inside the frame; again, use the 6.3mm straight cutter.

The panel is made from thinner material. Rather than buy ready-made thinner stock, I reduced the 18mm panels to 12mm on a thicknesser — leaving it 3.7mm too thick for the groove means a rebate can be routed on the back to make it fit. A thicker panel will be less likely to split and will help to eliminate wind — twisting like a propeller — from the door.

Machine the rebate around the back of the panel using a bearing-guided rebate cutter, then soften the edge by running a decorative cove onto the step of the rebate.

Add interest to the front of the door by running a stopped chamfer on the inside of the

frame with a bearing-guided chamfer cutter. To mark out, dry assemble the doors and lightly mark a pencil line 10mm back from each of the inside corners; these marks indicate where the chamfer will stop.

Glue and cramp the door components together, keeping the panel glue-free to allow for movement.

Finish off by running the bearing-guided ogee cutter around the edge of the door.

Fit the door to the carcass using cabinet hinges. Follow the manufacturer's measuring instructions, or resort to trial and error on scrap wood.

Doubling up

Make two of the base units to create a desk or dressing table. The units are joined together by a rail front and back to support the top over the open span. The front rail is cut out and chamfered.

Battens screwed to the underside locate a large or small top onto the two cabinets. ●

Cutting list

	Carcass	wide	long	thick
2 off	Sides	465	715	18
1 off	Floor	445	383	18
1 off	Back	650	383	18
1 off	Top rail	55	383	18
1 off	Skirting	100	1500	18
Drawer				
2 off	Sides	148	350	18
2 off	Front and back	148	328	18
1 off	Drawer front	200	397	18
Door				
2 off	Stiles	65	400	18
2 off	Top and bottom	65	307	18
1 off	Panel	288	293	12
Top				
1 off	Bedside cabinet	500	430	18
1 off	Desk/dressing table	500	1340	18
	Desk/dressing table			
2 off	Joining rails	100	500	18

All measurements in millimetres

Bed and boards

MAKER

Anthony Bailey

In the first article of a three-part project **Anthony Bailey** uses Jesada cutters to make a headboard and matching footboard for a bed

O VER this and the following articles I shall be producing a double bed and under-drawer in pine, a great material that can be finished in its natural colour. In this case I may be tempted to try my hand at a hand-decorated paint finish.

This first part of the project involves making the existing headboard and adding a matching footboard, and these can be attached to a standard divan-type bed. In the next article I will be making the parts that will join the head and footboard together to make it into a bed in its own right that only requires a mattress. I have made this project to suit a double mattress but an adjustment in the measurements is all that is required to make a bed to suit any size of mattress.

▲ *A head and footboard will enhance a divan bed, or can be made into a bed in their own right*

"An adjustment in the measurements is all that is required to make a bed to suit any size of mattress"

▲ *Mark the positions of all the mortices*

Marking up

Firstly, measure the bed accurately, both the divan base and the mattress on top; determine the position of the solid frame inside the base because you will need to fix the head and footboards by screwing through and into them. Note how the tongue and groove 'V' (TGV) infill is the same height for both headboard and footboard, although the footboard itself is lower and the headboard has an additional rail to allow for fixing into the divan base. Using the same amount of TGV unifies the design and simplifies setting out. The tongue and groove is 'V'-moulded on both faces to look the same from both sides – not strictly necessary with the headboard.

Each frame has mortice and tenon joints, and the TGV is let into a narrow groove all round. Prepared softwood is used throughout. Start by cutting all four legs, then mark the rail positions on one leg, followed by the mortices.

These are 14mm (⁹⁄₁₆in) wide, and are 15mm (⅝in) less in height at both top and bottom for each rail except for the narrow rails where they are reduced to 10mm (⅜in) at the very top and very bottom; this avoids having to remove too much of the tenon on these narrower pieces. Now transfer these markings directly onto the other legs. A large router with two fences and a 12.7mm straight cutter is needed.

"As heating of the shank takes place I would advise that you use the cutter with the longest cutting edge possible"

▲ *A pair of side-fences are useful to stop the router from wandering*

▼ *Rout a central groove for the TGV tongues*

▶ *The three stages of creating TGV*

Cutting mortices

I based my choice of cutters on the comprehensive Jesada Router Magic Bit Set, but as long as the relevant cutters are to hand the make is irrelevant.

I thought I had all the required cutters, only realising when I came to cut these mortices that I was short of a long and strong, straight bit!

Using instead the set's 12.7mm cutter – which is the same size as the shank – I plunged it until the shank entered the hole and achieved the required 40mm (1⅝in) depth of cut.

This technique may sound far from ideal, but this happens with some pocket or mortice cutters anyway. As heating of the shank takes place I would advise that

you use the cutter with the longest cutting edge possible.

Using a pair of side-fences prevents the router from wandering when cutting the mortices. Set the cutter to line up with one side of the mortice, machine, then lift the router off, turn it round and cut the other way to create a 14mm (⁹⁄₁₆in) wide socket, which I made 40mm (1⅝in) deep.

Once all the processes of TGV have been achieved a Stanley knife can be used to clean up the fluffy end grain

Dry-fit the frames together to check how much TGV is required

"This groove must be deep enough to take the tongue on each outer piece of TGV"

Rails, tenons

Once all mortices are done, machine a 6mm (¼in) groove centrally and 8mm (⁵⁄₁₆in) deep from one mortice to the other – excluding the bottom-most rail on the headboard.

This groove must be deep enough to take the tongue on each outer piece of TGV.

Cut all rails to length and, on the router table, form tenons which are just shorter than the mortice sockets – say 38mm (1½in).

Use a mitre protractor and a backing piece to prevent tearing on the back face. Machine the flat faces, reset the cutter height and stand the rails on edge, doing the 10mm (⅜in) set backs, first and then resetting to accomplish the 15mm (⅝in) ones – this order avoiding mistakes!

Round the mortice corners with a chisel until they fit the sockets; you should aim for a snug fit that will allow for glue. At this point dry fit the full frame assemblies and check what length the TGV will need to be, excluding the tongues.

Close-up of the boards when fitted into the head and footboard frames

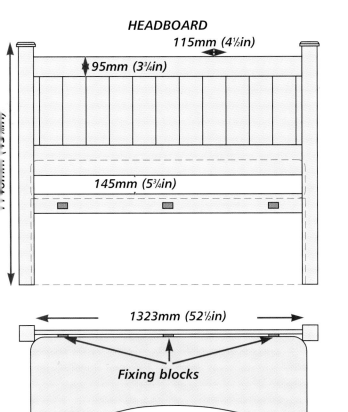

HEADBOARD

115mm (4½in)

95mm (3¾in)

145mm (5¾in)

1323mm (52½in)

Fixing blocks

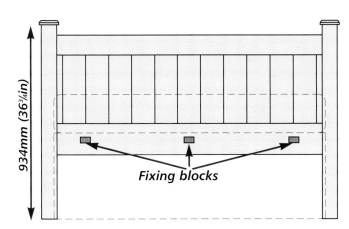

FOOTBOARD

934mm (36¾in)

Fixing blocks

Dotted line = outline of divan bed and mattress

▲ **Dimensions of the head and footboards**

Grooving rails

Now fit a grooving cutter in the table mounted router. Jesada do a neat set of groovers with one arbor, bearing and spacers.

Disassemble the frames and groove one long edge of all the rails to a depth of 15mm – except the base rail on the headboard – ready to receive a tongue when assembled.

The creation of TGV requires three separate cuts to prepare it. Start by forming the grooves on one long edge of each only — if you have already cut the blanks to length they will run flatter against the fence.

After ensuring that the groove is central and about 8mm (⁵⁄₁₆in) deep, fit a large-diameter straight cutter and form the matching tongues on the opposite edge as if making very thin tenons.

After checking for a neat fit, 'V' groove all four long edges. Tongue the ends of each TGV section, taking care not to make the tongues longer than about 13mm (½in), otherwise a gap will show top and bottom once assembled into the frame.

Assembly

With as many TGV sections fitted as possible, assemble both frames to check the fit. Push these tightly to one end and measure the resulting gap.

Divide this figure in two to find the

widths of the two missing pieces needed to fill in the gap at each end of the frame.

On one side a groove and a new tongue are needed; on the other an extra tongue is formed. As one new one is required add on the extra tongue width. There is room for a mistake here, so have some spare pieces just in case.

Take each frame apart again and apply glue to the tenons which go into one leg. Assemble this end of the frame, then put in a narrow piece of TGV followed by all the rest of the TGV and finishing up with the other narrow piece, so achieving a balanced look.

Glue the other leg on and, after ensuring

that the whole frame is square, cramp it up. If necessary apply some cramps from top to bottom of the frame so that the rails close tightly against the TGV.

Finally, make up some caps to go on top of the legs, cut them to size and bevel them around the top edge with the 'V' cutter, then glue and pin them on.

Because the legs would stop the rails sitting tightly against the bed base, make up some strips to screw on the base and into the rails.

In the following article I show how, with the addition of frame and slats, the headboard and footboard can be converted to make a complete bed, without the need for a divan base. ●

"There is room for a mistake here, so have some spare pieces just in case"

A nice finishing touch is the bevelled caps on top of the legs

Making connections

MAKER

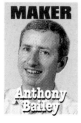

Anthony Bailey

Anthony Bailey adds frame and slats to his bed project

I N the last article I showed you how to make a pine tongue-and-groove headboard and footboard for attaching to a divan-type double bed. This article deals with converting the headboard and footboard, by machining the bedposts to allow the attachment of the side rails, making a replacement frame and slats, and thereby creating a complete bed without the need for a divan base.

An essential ingredient is a means of fitting the frames together which is demountable and does not depend on complicated jointwork.

Bed connectors are ideal, obtainable from specialist suppliers like Häfele, Tradecraft Supplies or Isaac Lord, *see page 102 for contact details.*

Start by obtaining some decent softwood, and check it is true along its length as the bed side rails, centre support and the slats must not be bowed.

The two wide side pieces not only couple the head and footboard together but also have a 50 by 25mm (2 by 1in) rail running along the inside for the slats to lie on.

Tooling up

- Small router
- Fence
- Jesada 16mm straight bit
- Jesada 6.4mm straight cutter
- Jesada 45° cutter

"Check that the height mark is the same on all four posts by marking the height on a stick – also known as a rod – and using this to avoid mistakes"

The slats of a double bed must be supported centrally – unnecessary with a single – and this is achieved by notched blocks fitted at each end of the bed.

Connectors, posts
Cut the bed side rails to length, then prepare to machine the recesses for the bed connectors.

The Häfele bed connectors I used couldn't be simpler. Made of plain steel, the more load that is put on them,

▲ *An attractive bed completed*

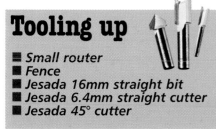

the better they lock together.

Because they don't come as left- and right-hand fittings, the only critical position is the bottom of the tapered slots in the receiving half. The hook-in part of the connector sits here when coupled.

Assuming the side rails of the bed will be centred on the head and footboard posts, draw the rail section on the post to see exactly where the receiving part of the connector will be situated.

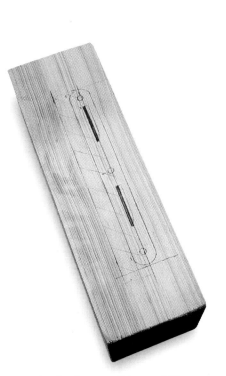

▲ *Mark the position of the receiving plates on the bed's legs; use an offcut for setting up the cutter and to use as a test piece for fitting the two components together*

▼ *Rout the housing for the receiving plate; note the length of the deeper central slot allows for the hooks*

▲ *Make up a template to rout the housings in the side rails*

"Ensure that the slot goes down the post further than the opening in the steel plate as the hooks will slide downward to engage"

Check that the height mark is the same on all four posts by marking the height on a stick – also known as a rod – and using this to avoid measuring mistakes.

The hook part of the connector will be set flush into the inside face of each side rail so you can align the receiving part, centring it for height, with the rail. It is in fact offset to one side although the amount is slightly different between the left- and right-hand bedposts.

Draw around the plate with a sharp pencil, then, using a router fitted with a side-fence and a 16mm straight bit installed, make the slot in one pass. To set the plate in flush make the cut just over 2mm (³⁄₃₂in) deep, the same thickness as the plate.

The two narrower, deeper slots needed to take the hook part are cut with a 6.4mm straight cutter; ensure that the slot is machined down the post further than the opening in the steel plate as the hooks will

▼ *The plates in place ready to fit together*

slide downward to engage.

The other half of the connector must be set in flush with the inside face of the side rail and is centred for height.

A template is necessary as the ends have a curved shape and must look neat. A 16mm guidebush with 6.4mm cutter works well and produces a good fit.

Make up the two notched blocks for the central support rail, a nominal 300mm long by 10mm wide (12 by ⅜in). Cut their 60mm (2⅜in) high notches centrally, just wide enough for the 10 by 25mm (⅜ by 1in) centre support to fit snugly. Bevel for a better finish.

Slat rails, slats

Fit the two halves of each connector, assemble the bed then screw on the slat support rails and the notched blocks.

I set the slat rails down just enough for the slats to end up about 6 to 8mm (¼ to ⅝₆in) below the top edge of the side rails. This allows the notched block on the head-board to be fitted at the same height as the separate lower rail of the headboard.

Screw on the slat rails at each end and check they are level all along; if not, push the rail up or down in the middle before driving a screw home to hold it level, then secure it using more screws in between.

Measure the centre slat support and cut it to length, then, with a handsaw, saw the ends to fit in the notches so it is flush with the top.

▲ *The side rails have a batten attached to the inside to support the slats*

▼ *A central support rail for the slats fits into a slotted plate*

▲ Slats are held in position by stapling seat webbing to them; they are spaced apart with an offcut

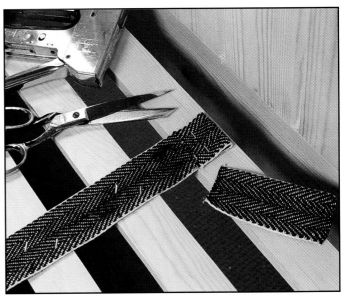

▲ Tidy the ends of the webbing by folding over and stapling

Now measure the gap between the rails at both ends of the bed and the middle. Any slight bow in or out in the centre can be eliminated later, *see below*, by screwing down the middle slats.

Cut the bed slats to fit neatly between the side rails. The number of slats is determined by the gap between them, which should be about the same as the width of each slat.

Assuming 21 slats each of 45.5mm (1²⁵⁄₃₂in) finished width – I used a calculator to work that out! – I found that I would have a gap between the slats of 45mm (1¾in) – close enough.

With the slats carefully spaced, run two strips of upholstery webbing over them and staple the webbing with an industrial-quality stapler.

Tension and staple the webbing to each end of the bed and then gap the slats accurately with the aid of a spare 50 by 25mm (2 by 1in) piece of slat timber.

Shoot two 12mm staples diagonally into each slat before moving on to the next – don't be tempted to put in all the staples on one side first as the results may be uneven.

Release the webbing from the bed ends, trim and staple over the webbing ends, roll up the slats and turn them over so the webbing and the staples are on the underside.

Pull the whole lot out flat and put the mattress on. The slats will stay put without further fixing, but now is the time to screw down one or two middle slats if necessary to hold the two side rails the correct distance apart, *see above*.

Finally, apply your choice of finish to the whole bed.

The bed is now complete, but could take a roll-out storage drawer, if desired, and I'll be making that in the next article. ●

▲ The addition of side rails and slats finishes the bed which now awaits a coat of varnish or paint – and some bedding of course

"The number of slats is determined by the gap between them, which should be about the same as the width of each slat"

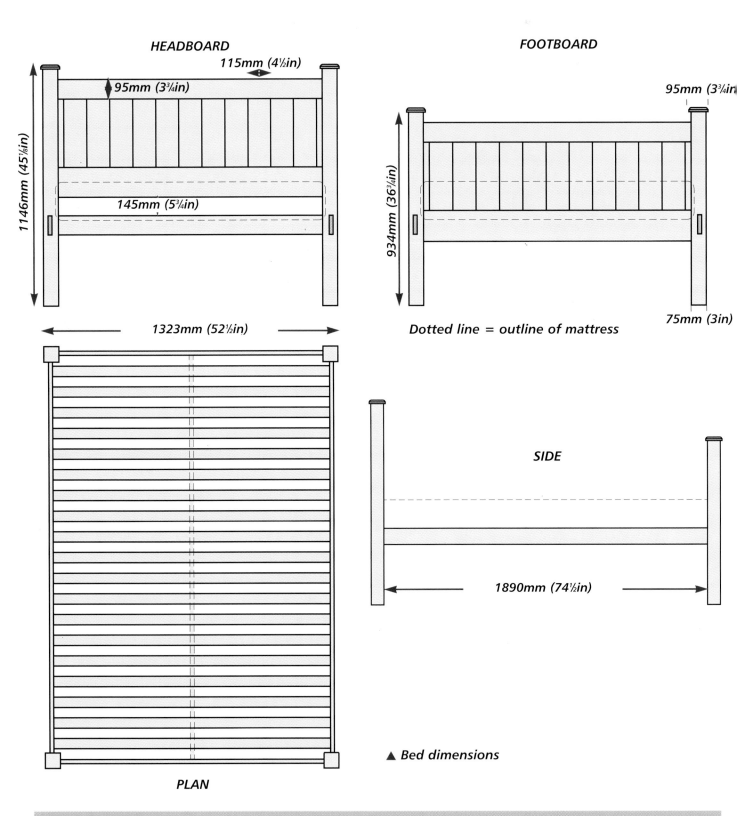

HEADBOARD

FOOTBOARD

115mm (4½in)

95mm (3¾in)

95mm (3¾in)

1146mm (45⅛in)

934mm (36¾in)

145mm (5¾in)

75mm (3in)

Dotted line = outline of mattress

1323mm (52½in)

SIDE

1890mm (74½in)

▲ Bed dimensions

PLAN

Suppliers

Häfele UK Ltd, Swift Valley Industrial Estate, Rugby, Warwickshire CV21 1RD, tel 01788 542020, fax 01788 544440.

Tradecraft Supplies, Country Gardens, London Road, Windlesham, Surrey GU20 6LL, tel 01344 876955, fax 01344 873862.

Isaac Lord, Unit 5 Desborough Industrial Park, Desborough Park Road, High Wycombe, Bucks HP12 3BX, tel 01494 459191, fax 01494 461376.

Яussian

under the bed

MAKER
Anthony Bailey

In the final part of the bed project **Anthony Bailey** makes and fits a drawer

A large drawer is the perfect complement to the bed

To complete my bed project, covered in the two preceding articles, I am making a drawer to go under the bed.

The bottom of the drawer is light-coloured Russian birch ply and the front, back and sides are in pine to match the bed.

For simplicity, I have chosen to have one drawer at the footboard end of the bed, which will run on heavy-duty industrial-type castors.

Making wide boards

The drawer front comes up higher than the front of the frame, so the gap between them is concealed. There is a close, neat, fit between the bed posts, and as the drawer side width is a fraction narrower than the front, the drawer slides smoothly between the legs.

The first job is to make boards wide enough for all the components. Softwood often isn't available in pieces of the correct

Tooling up

Jesada cutters used
- Glue joint cutter
- Slotter set
- 9.5mm straight cutter
- V-groover
- 45° chamfer cutter
- 12.7mm cove cutter

▲ *The glue joint cutter makes another appearance*

▲ *Grooves are formed for both the joint and drawer bottom*

width, so narrower pieces must be joined together. I used 120mm (4¾in) wide prepared boards which, when edge-jointed, can be cut down to width afterwards.

The best way to fit the boards together is to use a glue-joint cutter like the Jesada 655-501. This is more secure than a tongue-and-groove joint, and gives plenty of strength.

To even out any tendency to bow, make sure each alternate board has its annular rings lying the opposite way.

Set up the router table so the centre of the glue-joint cutter is centred on the board thickness. This ensures good flush faces when joined. If the cutter isn't centred it will cause a step which will need sanding out.

Also, use flat, unbowed boards, otherwise there will be a lot of mismatched edges.

"Brush-glue the edges and assemble the boards, holding them tightly in sash cramps"

There is no bearing on this cutter, but if you set the fence on the router table carefully, and do some test joints, tightly-jointed edges are easily produced.

I was lazy and machined the edges, turning each board over before doing the other edge. This meant I could choose which edges best fitted together, and allowed me to get the annular rings running alternately.

Having assembled each group of three boards, I sawed to width, taking

off the surplus glue-joint edges in the process.

Brush-glue the edges and assemble the boards, holding them tightly in sash cramps. Smears of glue would mark the surface and mean extra sanding out, so wash off the excess with a damp cloth and leave to dry.

Also, if the wood is to be stained the colour will not penetrate glue-smeared grain. Any sanding needed to level the boards' joints should be done now.

▼ *The slotting cutter set up to form the tongue*

▼ *The drawer's corner joint is designed to give maximum strength when pulled*

▲ V-grooves decorate the drawer's face

▲ A cove cutter creates the finger pull on the underside of the drawer front

▲ Sturdy castors are required to take the load

Corner jointing

Because this isn't a small cabinet drawer, I decided to use a simple tongue-and-groove joint for the corner jointing. This needs some care in setting up and machining.

Cut all the components to their respective widths and lengths. The drawer sides run from front to back, with a groove routed on their inside faces, both front and back. Machine a tongue on the ends of the front and back boards to lock into the side grooves.

The joint is produced this way so that any strain caused by pulling on the drawer front won't pull it right off; also, the highly visible drawer sides then look neat.

Make the front and back boards the measurement between the sides, plus about 9mm (⅜in) for each of the tongues.

Grooving, sanding

Next, set up the table to do the grooving. Cut a 9.5mm (⅜in full) wide groove in the drawer sides, then use the straight cutter to cut grooves on the bottom inside face of all the boards.

These grooves will take the 9mm (⅜in) ply drawer bottom, which needs to start

40mm (1⅝in) from the bottom edge of each board.

The groove is positioned so that the drawer sides and back come down a little over the castors to hide them as much as possible. There should be a 10mm (⅜in) exposure of castor on all sides.

I used the Jesada Slotter set to form the tongue. Since the groove depth needs to be 9mm (⅜in), I used the fence of the router table for guidance rather than the bearing.

The panels are too wide to use a mitre protractor to push them, so press the

"Some sandpaper on a block will remove marks from any type of sander"

▼ Fill the drawer up with blankets, sheets and all sorts of other stuff

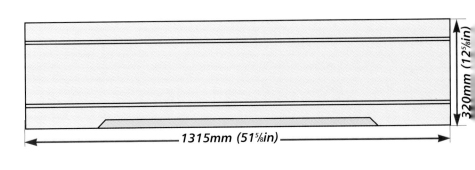

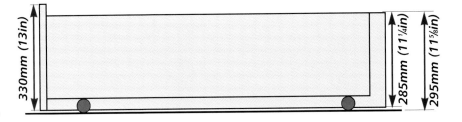

panel end against the fence and slide it past the cutter, holding a backing piece behind to avoid tear-out or spelching.

Sand all parts before assembly. I use a random orbital sander to reduce the amount of swirly rings that a conventional sander produces. However, a flick over, along the grain with some sandpaper on a block, will remove marks from any type of sander.

Cut the birch ply 2mm (⅟₁₆in) smaller than the overall distance between the deepest part of the side grooves.

With the front and back in place, glue and assemble the drawer, taking care to brush the glue onto the tongue before fitting into the slot. Use three 50mm (2in) panel pins per joint to hold them together, and punch them in for filling later.

"Don't wander or you'll take a chunk out of the edge!"

Drawer front

The drawer front is a separate item, and covers the joints on the front of the drawer box. Use a V-groover to create two deep grooves, each centred at 55mm (2⅛in) from each long edge, then use the V-groover or a chamfer 45° cutter with a bearing, to create two smaller bevels along the very edge, top and bottom.

Mark out the cut-out shape along the bottom edge. The bevelled ends to this cut-out are chosen to match the rest of the design.

Use a jigsaw or bandsaw, and clean up with abrasive paper. Invert the drawer front and use a 12.7mm cove cutter with a bearing to make a hand-grip shape along the edge of the cut-out.

Don't wander beyond this area, as the bevel on the front face will not give any support to the bearing, and you will take a chunk out of the edge!

Finally, screw the drawer front to the drawer box with the bottom edges flush, and any side overhang equalised. Fix the castors underneath near the corners using short fat screws.

Because this is an awesomely large drawer, you can fill it with blankets, woollies, crumpled shirts and whatever else you have, then push it under the bed and forget about everything in it! ●

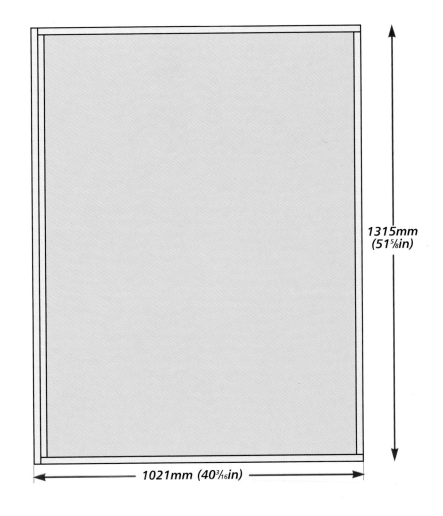

▲ **Dimensions of under-bed drawer**

The linenfold effect on the finished chest

Blanket coverage

TUTOR

Anthony Bailey

Anthony Bailey demonstrates that cheating's fine when the result is a beautiful copy of an early oak chest

English oak selected and machined ready for use

I JUMPED at the chance when the Editor asked me to make a blanket chest based on one featured in Ralph Fastnedge's book *English Furniture Styles*. Although I have made many pieces in English oak,

the disciplines of hand carving involved in achieving linenfold panelling always put me off.

But thanks to Wealden Cutters' new linenfold cutter set my excuses have run out. Wealden boss Alan Arnott

has designed cutter profiles which produce a convincingly effective substitute for the real thing.

My own substantial collection of cutters has been almost exclusively Wealden from the year dot, so I have

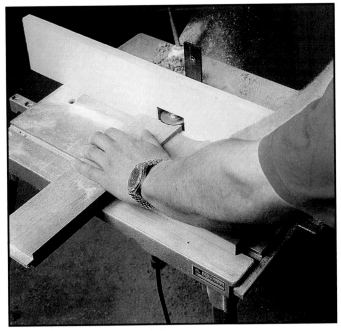

▲ *Cutting tongues on stiles*

▲ *Bottom piece showing tongues, leg cut-out and groove*

▲ *Stopped chamfers and cutter*

no hesitation in recommending them. Equivalent cutters made by other companies can be used for all the operations in this project except, of course, the linenfold work.

Flighty oak

Because oak is a wasteful timber with a flighty nature, purchase double the amount of timber required for the chest to allow for wastage.

For the dimensions of the chest I scaled off the drawing in the book, but it could be made to any size, remembering to keep it in proportion.

I used some thick air-dried, hurricane-felled oak and cut all the components oversize, planed them over-thickness and left the timber for some weeks to acclimatise before re-machining the pieces to the finished size.

Because this is meant to emulate an early piece of furniture with linenfold detail, the stock thickness needs to be 25mm (1in) for the stiles and rails and about 16 to 18mm ($^5/_8$ to $^3/_4$in) for the panels. The legs are made up of two pieces of 25mm (1in) oak to give the required thickness. I reserved the ray-figured boards for the linenfold panels.

To make construction easier treat each face of the chest as one complete item. The front and back and the lid comprise complete 'units', and the ends and bottom are fitted afterwards.

T & G cutters

Wealden's Shaker-style large tongue-and-groove (T & G) cutter set allows neat jointing and panelling without having to resort to mortice and tenons. A router table and a large router will be needed for this operation.

Calculation of component sizes is all important. Mark the square face sides and edges of the components when planing to size and work to these marks as a datum throughout the project to ensure flush joint faces.

Cut the stock for the legs and stiles somewhat over-length ready to be cut to size later on, but cut the rails and muntins exactly 24mm ($^{15}/_{16}$in) longer than the distance between the stiles or legs. This is to allow for a 12mm ($^{15}/_{32}$in) tongue each end to fit the depth of groove created by the T & G set.

The panels need to be about 2mm ($^5/_{64}$in) shorter than the rail, including tongue, so that when slid into the groove there is enough free play to allow for assembly.

The T & G set comes with shims to get the right fit, so it is sensible to make several trial joints first and mark the correct shim with a felt-tipped pen so that the right one is used.

Rout the scribing cuts first (the tongue) and then the profile (the groove). I did some of the grooves at full cut depth but found the 'ragging' of the edges unacceptable and swapped to 'pre-scoring' –

this means a first cut at about 2mm ($^5/_{64}$in) deep to give nice clean edges followed by a full 12mm ($^{15}/_{32}$in) pass which should remove the bulk of the material without disturbing those edges.

Because the panels need a slightly looser tongue a different shim is needed.

All the components for the end and base can be cut at the same time as the main ones, but on final assembly they might need slight re-machining.

Chamfers, grooves

The stopped chamfers on the lid frame are applied with a

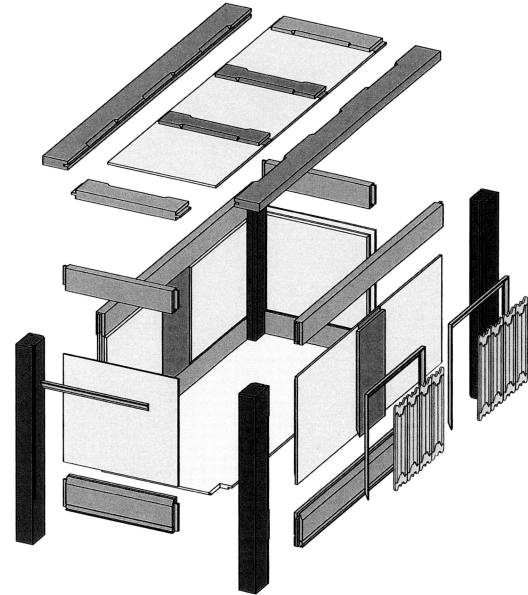

Bottom panel

Linenfold plaques

Panel moulding

Legs

Rails

Muntins

Stiles

Panels

▲ *Exploded view of linenfold chest*

"Don't bother to glue the base strips in place, as they must be allowed to shrink"

45° cutter, either using a fence on a router table or with the router hand-held working off the side fence. Ensure you have made pencil marks for the start and stop points and don't hold the wood in one place on the spinning cutter too long as doing so would result in a burn mark.

The panels are butt-glued together, then machined and sanded to a finish before assembly takes place. They are flat on the outside but project slightly on the inside of the chest due to their thickness. Use the same 45°

chamfer cutter to put a bevel on after tonguing their inside face.

Also before assembly rout large edge beads on the front of the lower rails and a groove on the reverse to take the chest bottom panel. To avoid breaking through the wood the groove should be higher than the bead.

The large chamfer running down the inside corner of the legs can either be done now or after the first glue up.

To make the routed small stopped edge bead look as if it has been achieved with

scratchstock, whittle each end of the cut with a chisel, and sand lightly.

Fitting frame

All of the frame parts should be sanded before assembly.

After a 'dry-fit' trial run, glue up the front, back and lid items separately with PVA or Cascamite and cramp up using sash cramps. Place paper between the cramps and the timber to avoid staining from the metal.

Leave to dry then trim the legs to finished length.

Lay the back of the chest down and dry-fit the end parts and the front on top of it.

The base, consisting of a series of planks, tongue-and-grooved all round and with the grain running from back to front, can then be cut to size.

Make cut-outs on the two

end planks to fit around the legs; place them in their groove each end of the chest. Then fill in between them with the rest of the planks, using a square and a scribe to mark the size.

Mark and cut each one individually until there is a small gap. Trim the last plank to a snug fit when the last tongue is machined.

Gluing, sanding

Now glue the whole chest together. Don't bother to glue the base strips in place, as they must be allowed to shrink. Use protective pads and sit the cramped up chest on a flat surface to make sure it is square – sight across the top to check if it is 'in wind' (twisted). If both ends are exactly in line there is no wind. If they are not, adjust

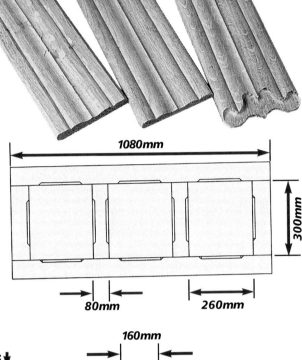

◀ **Linen fold strips in their various stages**

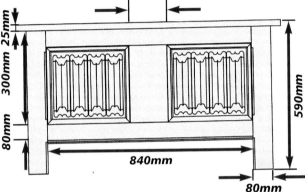

1080mm

300mm

80mm 260mm

160mm

25mm 300mm 80mm

840mm

590mm

80mm

450mm

70mm

320mm

50mm

▲ **Routing hinge sockets – note bar clamped to chest to provide router with a running surface**

Bailey's tips

Leaving glue to become 'plasticky' – but not set – makes cleaning up neater as it can be done with the second best chisel rather than by wiping and washing off the surplus, which raises the grain and can push glue into the pores of the wood. To get the amount of glue right, I favour using a slim wedge cut on the bandsaw as an applicator, or a dispenser with a spout.

When preparing the small mouldings use a wide board of the right thickness and machine one edge, cut it off on the saw and repeat as necessary – then sand carefully.

To avoid kickback when doing stopped cuts on the fence, apply the far end of the work against the fence, slowly swing the front end against it and feed the wood over the cutter.

by placing a small packer under one leg, then leave the glue to set overnight.

The 'horns' on the lid stiles can be trimmed to length then sanded all round. Then, with the box open in front of you, check that the lid fits and overhangs the front and sides correctly.

There may be a slight step where the frames are joined. This will need sanding flush, taking care to avoid the projecting bevelled panels. I worked over all outside frame surfaces and top edges with my 4in belt sander and sharp 120 grit.

Moulding frames

The front and back feature a plain bevel along and a classic profile panel moulding around the other three sides. The ends of the chest also have the bevel on the top of the bottom rail, but the moulding is applied only across the top. A narrow border will separate the linenfold plaques and panel mouldings.

Cut the mouldings with a mitre saw, then glue them

into place, holding with masking tape until dry. Note that the vertical pieces on the front and back are next to the edge bead so need to be rounded over with abrasive paper until they look right.

Lastly, remove sander scratches by running an orbital sander and 180 grit over the whole chest.

All arises (sharp edges) need to be taken off by hand with a quick flick of fine abrasive and the ends of the legs chamfered to reduce any carpet damage.

Linenfold process

Unlike the woodworkers who made early oak chests and panelling, thanks to Wealden we need only give passing concern to the linenfolding as it is machined as plaques and applied afterwards.

The plaques are made from stock 75mm (3in) wide and 10mm ($^3/_8$in) thick. When calculating the size of the chest make sure the panel sizes measure in multiples of 75mm (3in) plus the size of the border you need.

The prepared stock must be profiled in two passes as the cutter does one half of the width. Adjust the fence so that the second cut cleans up and the 'folding' needs only limited sanding.

Next, carefully cut the pieces to length using a table or radial arm saw; make sure more lengths than you need are cut in case some are imperfect. Unusually, the scribing cuts are done after the profiling.

Then make a jig which clamps the plaques and has a special profile at the end. In combination with the relevant cutters, this produces the full effect of the scribing cut. Wealden provide a full-size template for the jig which is transferred to the MDF or Tufnol jig material.

First, set the inverted plaque to one line and, using a straight profiling cutter with a bottom bearing, run along the shaped edge of the jig to scribe one half the width of the plaque.

Invert the plaque to shape the other half, then pull it

▲ *Routing internal chamfer on leg*

▲ *Fitting bottom pieces*

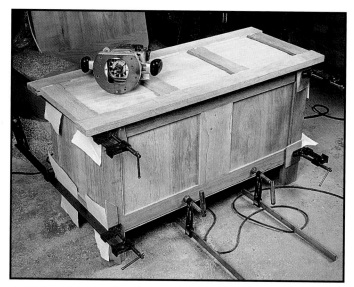

▲ *Main carcass glued up*

Tooling up

....

The following were used in this project:

Wealden Tool Co, Linenfold set, Large tongue and groove set, Chamfer T916B ¼ shank, V Groove T128 ¼ shank, Hinge morticing T310 ¼ shank, Panel trim T8018B ½ shank, beaded edge T2503B ¼ shank, T2504B ½ shank, Classic panel guided T1622B ¼ shank.

▲ *Wealden linenfold cutters and others used in the project*

back to the second marked line on the jig. With the small bearing guided cutter provided, move the router across the jig and clean off the top of the exposed area of the plaque, so producing a 'carved' effect at the end of each strip.

After a light sanding the plaques can be applied to the panels on the chest. I put an even layer of glue on the backs of four linenfold plaques, placed them on a blank panel and rubbed them gently into place – though a bit of gentle weighting down would be a good idea.

If you don't put glue near the edges, it shouldn't ooze out when the plaques are in place.

Sinking hinges

Mark positions on the back top rail for three 2½in brass butts. They will be sunk into the rail but not into the lid using the router with a 12 or 16mm diameter hinge mortice bit.

With the router stationary plunge it so the hinge mortice bit just touches a flat surface. Then place the thinnest part of the folded hinge between the depth stop and turret and lock the stop at that depth, lowering the stop a little more if the cut appears to be too deep.

Clamp a board against the top rail to give a larger surface and set the side fence on the router so the hinges will have half the 'knuckle' projecting from the rail. Now machine out the hinge slot, starting along the edge to avoid tear-out.

Cut carefully up to the end

Inside detail ▶

marks, then square out the corners with a sharp chisel. Screw on the lid then take it off again to apply the finish before replacing it.

Finishing

Apply by brush two coats of Liberon finishing oil to reach all the in-between bits, wait a short while and rub off to produce a gentle sheen. Then apply a coat of Liberon Black Bison clear wax for a soft feel and a pleasant smell. Lastly, rub down the hinges and screws with fine abrasive to get rid of the factory 'drawn' finish. ●

Mid-winter

MAKER
Guy Smith

Guy Smith makes a dream of a versatile folding screen

Not only can this relatively simple to make dressing screen serve several purposes, but its method of construction is also ideal for doors and panelled carcassing.

Choice of timber is up to the individual, and I opted for softwood with a plywood panel as both these materials readily accept paint. They are also relatively light, which makes the screen far more manoeuvrable.

If you are not able to prepare the wood yourself then it can be purchased, prepared, from a timber merchant, but it is always advisable to select your own wood in order to ensure that it is as straight and flawless as possible.

Router table

For safety and accuracy, all the jointing is performed on a router inversion table, constructed from a piece of sheet material approximately 500 to 600mm square and at least 18mm thick.

Mark a line about 250mm back from the front edge, mark the half-way point along this line and then drill through, using a flat bit — 35mm should suffice for most cutters. This hole allows the cutter to be plunged up through the table.

Next, position a router on the table with the spindle centralised over the hole. Mark the points at which the router baseplate is threaded to receive fixing bolts, then drill them in the table and countersink from the top so the bolt heads don't protrude.

Bolt the router onto the underside of the table and it's ready to be screwed or cramped to the workbench.

Incorporating a mobile extraction unit or an old vacuum cleaner into the fence will take care of any chippings or dust.

Grooves

Set the fence and use a 9mm straight cutter to rout a groove centrally on the inside edges of the stiles, the top rail and on both edges of the middle and bottom rails. This groove will accommodate both the panels and the tenons.

The groove on the underside of the bottom rail will later accommodate the bracket foot. Rout to a depth of 15mm in several cuts, reducing their size if the cutter chatters.

Cutting tenons

To cut the tenons in the top, middle and bottom rails, use a larger 12 or 18mm straight cutter, place one of the grooved components flat on the table and raise the cutter so the end is flush with the edge of the groove.

▲ *Set the depth of the cutter to the groove and machine the tenon's first cut*

Machine a few practice pieces to obtain the correct depth setting.

The tenon is machined to length in two passes, so first set the fence to allow 6 to 8mm of the cutter to protrude in front of it.

A notch cut in the fence will allow the cutter to rotate freely. This can be achieved either by removing the fence and routing it, or by lightly cramping one end of the fence to the table of the inversion stand and moving the fence across the cutter slowly until it has cut its own housing.

Make this cut a little deeper than it needs to be, then back it off a bit so that the cutter is not in constant contact with the fence.

Then rout the ends of the rails, passing them across the cutter. Use of a square of waste material behind the workpiece avoids break-out and helps keep the rails square to the fence. Turn the workpiece over and repeat the process on the other side.

Move the fence back to machine the finished shoulder cut of the tenons to a depth of 15mm and repeat the process.

Bracket feet

Whilst set up for this operation, the bracket feet can be machined in the same way on two edges, allowing them to be slotted into the groove on the bottom rail and stile. As the feet are 5mm thinner than the rest of the stock the depth of cut will have to be reduced. The feet can then be cut to shape and sanded.

The router table is also used when the cove moulding is applied to the edge and

▲ *A simple router table screwed to the bench for light duty work*

▲ *Routing the groove for tenons and panels*

ght's screen

▲ *Move the fence back to cut the tenon 15mm long on both sides; use a piece of sheet material to keep the workpiece square*

"For safety and accuracy, all the jointing is performed on a router inversion table"

radius of the foot. Because the feet are quite small and tricky to hold, it is necessary to use a small batten attached to the foot in order to machine it safely.

A rebate along one side of the batten allows the batten to be hooked over the shoulder of the tenon on the back of the foot and fixed by a couple of suitably sized panel pins.

This ensures good control over the workpiece as well as keeping your valued pinkies away from the cutter.

Before cutting the cove with a 13mm bearing-guided cove cutter, elevate the cutter slightly so only the guide bearing is exposed, then practise passing the foot around the bearing with the router switched off until confident that an even pressure can be applied on the workpiece during the process.

Once happy, cut the moulding in a couple

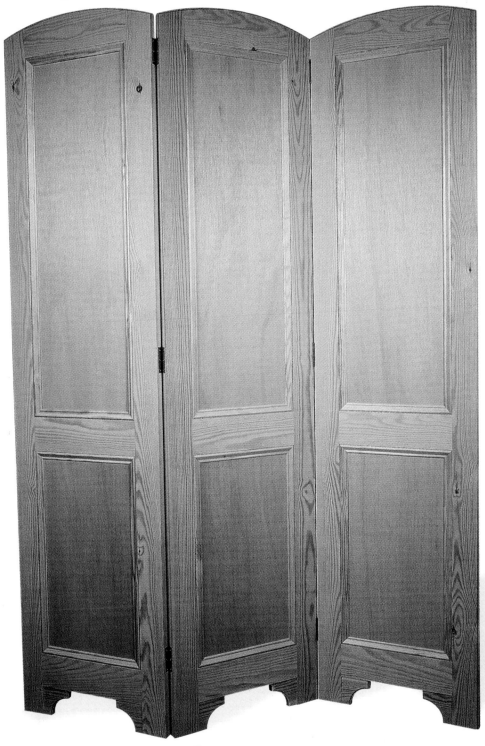

▲ *Exploded view of folding screen*

▲ *Re-set the depth of the cutter and machine the tenons on the feet*

▲ *Use a batten pinned to the feet to rout the decorative cove*

▲ *The batten is essential to keep fingers away from the cutter when routing the cove on the ends of the feet*

▲ *The screen components ready to assemble*

◀ *A plywood panel will need a clearance of only 0.5mm all round*

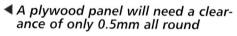

Someone ▶ *saucy slipping behind the screen*

of cuts rather than run the risk of the cutter grabbing or burning the timber. Give the feet their final sanding before assembly.

Panels

Cut the panels to the required size, allowing approximately 0.5mm all round to ensure all the joints can close up fully.

Allow about 1.5mm each side to allow for timber expansion and fix the panel in position with a spot of glue in the centre of the panel top and bottom, allowing it to expand outwards from the centre while stopping it rattling around within the frame.

Assembly

With all the components prepared, the three screens are ready to be glued up.

Mark the position of the top, middle and bottom rails on to the stiles and assemble accordingly, either cramping them together or by using screws and end-grain plugs.

Check to ensure everything is flat and

▲ *Using a jig to rout the curved heads*

Tooling up

- ■ *35mm flat bit*
- ■ *9mm straight-fluted cutter*
- ■ *12 or 18mm straight-fluted cutter*
- ■ *13mm bearing-guided cove cutter*
- ■ *30mm guide bush*

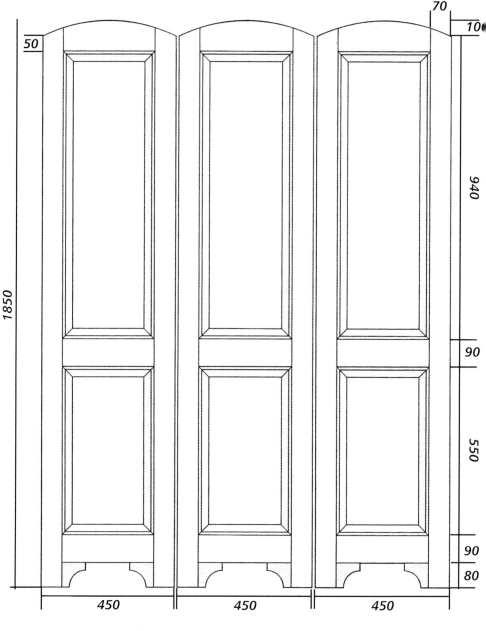

▲ *Folding screen dimensions*

square across the diagonals, and that excess glue from the joints is not making its way into the space for the panel.

After assembly, clean up the joints and glue the feet into the groove in the bottom rail and stile, and hold in place with G-cramps — masking tape is perfectly adequate if the joints are good.

Curved heads

To machine the curve on the top of the screen, simply take a piece of ply 9 by 550 by 150mm — the 50mm extra each end ensures a smooth run on and off the work. Mark and cut it to your chosen radius then sand it smooth.

This jig can now be placed onto the top rail of the screens and the curve marked onto them; jigsaw the curve to within 1 to 2mm outside the pencil line.

To rout the curve using the jig I chose a 30mm guide bush in conjunction with an 18mm cutter. The difference between the outside edge of the cutter and that of the collar is 6mm.

Move the jig 6mm back from its original position, clamp it in position and rout the curve, running the guide bush on the edge of the jig. To avoid break-out at the end of the cut a block of wood can be held on to the stile from underneath with a sash cramp.

Mouldings

Moulding applied to the outside front edges of the frames will lighten the appearance of the piece. Again I have chosen to maintain the same theme as the feet by using the 13mm cove cutter with guide bearing.

Do not apply this moulding to the inside edges of the screen where they are to be hinged together. Either cut in butt hinges using a router to machine the housing and clean up the corners by hand with a chisel, or use quick and easy lay-on hinges.

Before attaching the hinges, give the screens a final sand and remove any sharp edges. A decorative moulding can now be mitred and applied to the panels; either rout your own profile or purchase one of the many patterns available off-the-shelf. To ensure all joints will sit down flush with

one another, take a small chamfer off the back edge of the mitres with a craft knife or chisel.

The dressing screen is now ready to be hinged together and given the finish of your choice. Mine will end up painted, with stencils applied to match the curtains.

Now all I have to do is find someone saucy to slip behind it — oh well, I can always dream! ●

Component list

6 off stiles	*25 by 70 by 1850*
3 off top rails	*25 by 100 by 340*
3 off middle rails	*25 by 90 by 340*
3 off bottom rails	*25 by 90 by 340*
6 off bracket feet	*20 by 95 by 95*
3 off top panels	*970 by 340 by 9*
3 off bottom panels	*580 by 340 by 9*

All finished sizes in millimetres

Metric/Imperial Conversion Chart

mm	inch	mm	inch	mm	inch	mm	inch
1	0.03937	26	1.02362	60	2.36220	310	12.20472
2	0.07874	27	1.06299	70	2.75590	320	12.59842
3	0.11811	28	1.10236	80	3.14960	330	12.99212
4	0.15748	29	1.14173	90	3.54330	340	13.38582
5	0.19685	30	1.18110	100	3.93700	350	13.77952
6	0.23622	31	1.22047	110	4.33070	360	14.17322
7	0.27559	32	1.25984	120	4.72440	370	14.56692
8	0.31496	33	1.29921	130	5.11811	380	14.96063
9	0.35433	34	1.33858	140	5.51181	390	15.35433
l0	0.39370	35	1.37795	150	5.90551	400	15.74803
11	0.43307	36	1.41732	160	6.29921	410	16.14173
12	0.47244	37	1.45669	170	6.69291	420	16.53543
13	0.51181	38	1.49606	180	7.08661	430	16.92913
14	0.55118	39	1.53543	190	7.48031	440	17.32283
15	0.59055	40	1.57480	200	7.87401	450	17.71653
16	0.62992	41	1.61417	210	8.26771	460	18.11023
17	0.66929	42	1.65354	220	8.66141	470	18.50393
18	0.70866	43	1.69291	230	9.05511	480	18.89763
19	0.74803	44	1.73228	240	9.44881	490	19.29133
20	0.78740	45	1.77165	250	9.84252	500	19.68504
21	0.82677	46	1.81102	260	10.23622		
22	0.86614	47	1.85039	270	10.62992		
23	0.90551	48	1.88976	280	11.02362		
24	0.94488	49	1.92913	290	11.41732		
25	0.98425	50	1.96850	300	11.81102		

1 mm = 0.03937 inch
1 cm = 0.3937 inch
1 m   = 3.281 feet
1 inch = 25.4 mm
1 foot = 304.8 mm
1 yard = 914.4 mm

Imperial/Metric Conversion Chart

inch		mm	inch		mm	inch		mm
0	0	0	23/64	0.359375	9.1281	45/64	0.703125	17.8594
1/64	0.015625	0.3969				23/32	0.71875	18.2562
1/32	0.03125	0.7938	3/8	0.375	9.5250	47/64	0.734375	18.6531
3/64	0.046875	1.1906	25/64	0.390625	9.9219			
1/16	0.0625	1.5875	13/32	0.40625	10.3188	3/4	0.750	19.0500
			27/64	0.421875	10.7156			
5/64	0.078125	1.9844				49/64	0.765625	19.4469
3/32	0.09375	2.3812	7/16	0.4375	11.1125	25/32	0.78125	19.8438
7/64	0.109375	2.7781	29/64	0.453125	11.5094	51/64	0.796875	20.2406
			15/32	0.46875	11.9062	13/16	0.8125	20.6375
1/8	0.125	3.1750	31/64	0.484375	12.3031			
9/64	0.140625	3.5719				53/64	0.828125	21.0344
5/32	0.15625	3.9688	1/2	0. 500	12.700	27/32	0.84375	21.4312
11/64	0.171875	4.3656	33/64	0.515625	13.0969	55/64	0.858375	21.8281
			17/32	0.53125	13.4938			
3/16	0.1875	4.7625	35/64	0.546875	13.8906	7/8	0.875	22.2250
13/64	0.203125	5.1594	9/16	0.5625	14.2875	57/64	0.890625	22.6219
7/32	0.21875	5.5562				29/32	0. 90625	23.0188
15/64	0.234375	5.9531	37/64	0.578125	14.6844	59/64	0.921875	23.4156
1/4	0.250	6.3500	19/32	0.59375	15.0812			
			39/64	0.609375	15.4781	15/16	0.9375	23.8125
17/64	0.265625	6.7469				61/64	0.953125	24.2094
9/32	0.28125	7.1438	5/8	0.625	15.8750	31/32	0.96875	24.6062
19/64	0.296875	7.5406	41/64	0.640625	16.2719	63/64	0.984375	25.0031
5/16	0.3125	7.9375	21/32	0.65625	16.6688			
			43/64	0.671875	17.0656			
21/64	0.1328125	8.3344						
11/32	0.34375	8.7312	11/16	0.6875	17.4625			

l inch = 1.000 = 25.40 mm

Index

adhesives
  Cascamite 5, 109
  double-sided tape 79
  epoxy resin 64–5
  Evostick Resin W 5, 26
  hot-melt glue 78–9
  PVA 18, 43, 47, 71, 81, 109
  superglue 18, 57
  tips for using 110
  Titebond 5, 11, 17–18
  white glue 57–8
Adsett, Bob 31–5
arch, architectural 48–52

Bailey, Anthony 36–9, 69–77, 93–111
baize, applying 17
bed
  drawer to fit under 103–6
  frame & slats 98–102
  head- & footboard 93–7
bedside cabinet 87–92
biscuit cutters, Trend 11, 25, 43
blanket chest 107–11
boards
  chipboard 26
  hardboard 11, 54, 79
  MDF 11–12, 17–18, 25–6, 35–7, 44–5, 51,
    53–4, 61, 69–70, 73, 76, 82, 85, 110
  plywood 7, 11–12, 17, 22, 25–6, 29, 51–3,
    85, 90, 103, 106, 112
box, trinket 83–6
breadbox 10–14

cabinet
  bedside 87–92
  display 65–8
Cain, Bill 2–5, 10–19, 43–7
candle sconce 36–9
carving templates, Trend 83, 86
chest, blanket 107–11
chopping block, kitchen 6–9
clock face 53–9
coffee table 43–7
columns, fluted 48–52

condiment holder 2–5
Constanduros, Mark 6–9
Cox, Jack 53–8, 78–82
Curran, Bob 59–64
cutters
  Axminster Power Tools 18
  Forstner bits 4, 86
  Jesada 95, 97, 104–5
  Sears Craftsman 11
  Titman 11, 18
  Trend 89
  Wealden 25, 72, 107–8
cutlery tray 15–19

delivery problems overcome 22
dining table, extending 26–30
display cabinet 65–8
door
  cabinet 90, 92
  stable 31–5
draining board 24–5
drawer
  cabinet 90
  cutlery tray for 15–19
  kitchen 7–8
  under-bed 103–6
drills, Trend 25

Eden-Eadon, Colin 24–5, 35
extending dining table 26–30

Fastnedge, Ralph 107
finishes
  lacquer 42, 45
  oil 5, 14, 19, 25, 42, 68, 111
  polyurethane 9, 23, 42, 64
  Ronseal 30
  Rustin 58
  wax 19, 30, 68, 111
fireplace surround 69–72
folding screen 112–16
foot- & headboard for a bed 93–7

Goodsell, Alan 87–92

grain filler 30
grilles, decorative 75

Häfele bed connectors 98
Hall, Ian 65–8
hand mirror 78–82
head- & footboard for a bed 93–7

inlays 55–8, 80, 82

kitchen
  drainer 24–5
  stool 20–3
  trolley & chopping block 6–9

lamination 59, 79–80
lampstand, adjustable two-arm 59–64
lime paste, using 45
linenfold panelling 107–111
loose-tongue joints 42

McKeggie, Betty & Bill 20–3
Mackenzie, Dave 6, 9
mirror
  candleholder 36–9
  frame 40–2
  hand 78–82
mortice & tenon cutting 6–7, 22, 31–2,
  45–6, 65–8, 95–6, 112

Ninham, Lee 48–52

occasional table 43–7
Oliver, Les 26–30

parquetry 80–1
Phillips, Jim 83–6
picture frame 40–2
plug-makers, Trend 25

radiator covers 73–7
roll-top lid 11–12
router bits see cutters
router jigs, Trend 53, 78, 85–6

router tables
  Craft 83
  Elu 3, 10, 15
routers
  Bosch 26
  Elu 3, 10, 15, 18, 43, 55
  Ryobi 31
  Trend 86
safety measures 34, 90
salt & pepper holder 2–5
screen, folding 112–16
secret slot screw technique 30
Smith, Guy 112–16
Smith, Roger 40–2
stable door 31–5
stool, kitchen 20–3

table
  coffee 43–7
  extending dining 26–30
  occasional 43–7
timber
  ash 20, 40
  beech 8, 12, 24
  birch 17, 103, 106
  blackwood 57, 80
  cherry 26, 30
  ebony 57, 79–80
  mahogany 26, 83
  maple 24
  oak 2, 17–18, 43, 45, 59, 61, 108
  pear 65
  pine 6, 31, 38, 72, 87, 93, 98
  softwood 17, 40, 48, 51, 69, 98, 103, 112
  sycamore 10, 14, 24, 57, 80
  walnut, American black 78
tongue-and-groove cutting 33–4, 94–7, 108
trinket box 83–6
trolley, kitchen 6–9

veneer 26, 30, 57, 73, 80
vernier caliper 2, 15

wood dye 30

TITLES AVAILABLE FROM
GMC Publications
BOOKS

WOODCARVING

The Art of the Woodcarver	*GMC Publications*
Carving Birds & Beasts	*GMC Publications*
Carving on Turning	*Chris Pye*
Carving Realistic Birds	*David Tippey*
Decorative Woodcarving	*Jeremy Williams*
Essential Tips for Woodcarvers	*GMC Publications*
Essential Woodcarving Techniques	*Dick Onians*
Further Useful Tips for Woodcarvers	*GMC Publications*
Lettercarving in Wood: A Practical Course	*Chris Pye*
Power Tools for Woodcarving	*David Tippey*
Practical Tips for Turners & Carvers	*GMC Publications*
Relief Carving in Wood: A Practical Introduction	*Chris Pye*
Understanding Woodcarving	*GMC Publications*
Understanding Woodcarving in the Round	*GMC Publications*
Useful Techniques for Woodcarvers	*GMC Publications*
Wildfowl Carving – Volume 1	*Jim Pearce*
Wildfowl Carving – Volume 2	*Jim Pearce*
The Woodcarvers	*GMC Publications*
Woodcarving: A Complete Course	*Ron Butterfield*
Woodcarving: A Foundation Course	*Zoë Gertner*
Woodcarving for Beginners	*GMC Publications*
Woodcarving Tools & Equipment Test Reports	*GMC Publications*
Woodcarving Tools, Materials & Equipment	*Chris Pye*

WOODTURNING

Adventures in Woodturning	*David Springett*
Bert Marsh: Woodturner	*Bert Marsh*
Bill Jones' Notes from the Turning Shop	*Bill Jones*
Bill Jones' Further Notes from the Turning Shop	*Bill Jones*
Bowl Turning Techniques Masterclass	*Tony Boase*
Colouring Techniques for Woodturners	*Jan Sanders*
The Craftsman Woodturner	*Peter Child*
Decorative Techniques for Woodturners	*Hilary Bowen*
Essential Tips for Woodturners	*GMC Publications*
Faceplate Turning	*GMC Publications*
Fun at the Lathe	*R.C. Bell*
Further Useful Tips for Woodturners	*GMC Publications*
Illustrated Woodturning Techniques	*John Hunnex*
Intermediate Woodturning Projects	*GMC Publications*
Keith Rowley's Woodturning Projects	*Keith Rowley*
Make Money from Woodturning	*Ann & Bob Phillips*
Multi-Centre Woodturning	*Ray Hopper*
Pleasure and Profit from Woodturning	*Reg Sherwin*
Practical Tips for Turners & Carvers	*GMC Publications*
Practical Tips for Woodturners	*GMC Publications*

Spindle Turning	*GMC Publications*
Turning Green Wood	*Michael O'Donnell*
Turning Miniatures in Wood	*John Sainsbury*
Turning Pens and Pencils	*Kip Christensen and Rex Burningham*
Turning Wooden Toys	*Terry Lawrence*
Understanding Woodturning	*Ann & Bob Phillips*
Useful Techniques for Woodturners	*GMC Publications*
Useful Woodturning Projects	*GMC Publications*
Woodturning: Bowls, Platters, Hollow Forms, Vases, Vessels, Bottles, Flasks, Tankards, Plates	*GMC Publications*
Woodturning: A Foundation Course (New Edition)	*Keith Rowley*
Woodturning: A Fresh Approach	*Robert Chapman*
Woodturning: A Source Book of Shapes	*John Hunnex*
Woodturning Jewellery	*Hilary Bowen*
Woodturning Masterclass	*Tony Boase*
Woodturning Techniques	*GMC Publications*
Woodturning Tools & Equipment Test Reports	*GMC Publications*
Woodturning Wizardry	*David Springett*

WOODWORKING

40 More Woodworking Plans & Projects	*GMC Publications*
Bird Boxes and Feeders for the Garden	*Dave Mackenzie*
Complete Woodfinishing	*Ian Hosker*
David Charlesworth's Furniture-Making Techniques	*David Charlesworth*
Electric Woodwork	*Jeremy Broun*
Furniture & Cabinetmaking Projects	*GMC Publications*
Furniture Projects	*Rod Wales*
Furniture Restoration (Practical Crafts)	*Kevin Jan Bonner*
Furniture Restoration and Repair for Beginners	*Kevin Jan Bonner*
Furniture Restoration Workshop	*Kevin Jan Bonner*
Green Woodwork	*Mike Abbott*
Making & Modifying Woodworking Tools	*Jim Kingshott*
Making Chairs and Tables	*GMC Publications*
Making Fine Furniture	*Tom Darby*
Making Little Boxes from Wood	*John Bennett*
Making Shaker Furniture	*Barry Jackson*
Making Woodwork Aids and Devices	*Robert Wearing*
Minidrill: Fifteen Projects	*John Everett*
Pine Furniture Projects for the Home	*Dave Mackenzie*
Router Magic: Jigs, Fixtures and Tricks to Unleash your Router's Full Potential	*Bill Hylton*
Routing for Beginners	*Anthony Bailey*
The Scrollsaw: Twenty Projects	*John Everett*
Sharpening Pocket Reference Book	*Jim Kingshott*

Sharpening: The Complete Guide — *Jim Kingshott*
Space-Saving Furniture Projects — *Dave Mackenzie*
Stickmaking: A Complete Course — *Andrew Jones & Clive George*
Stickmaking Handbook — *Andrew Jones & Clive George*
Test Reports: *The Router* and *Furniture & Cabinetmaking* — *GMC Publications*
Veneering: A Complete Course — *Ian Hosker*
Woodfinishing Handbook (Practical Crafts) — *Ian Hosker*
Woodworking Plans and Projects — *GMC Publications*
Woodworking with the Router: Professional
Router Techniques any Woodworker can Use — *Bill Hylton & Fred Matlack*
The Workshop — *Jim Kingshott*
Seat Weaving (Practical Crafts) — *Ricky Holdstock*
The Upholsterer's Pocket Reference Book — *David James*
Upholstery: A Complete Course (Revised Edition) — *David James*
Upholstery Restoration — *David James*
Upholstery Techniques & Projects — *David James*

TOYMAKING

Designing & Making Wooden Toys — *Terry Kelly*
Fun to Make Wooden Toys & Games — *Jeff & Jennie Loader*
Making Board, Peg & Dice Games — *Jeff & Jennie Loader*
Making Wooden Toys & Games — *Jeff & Jennie Loader*
Restoring Rocking Horses — *Clive Green & Anthony Dew*
Scrollsaw Toy Projects — *Ivor Carlyle*
Scrollsaw Toys for All Ages — *Ivor Carlyle*
Wooden Toy Projects — *GMC Publications*

DOLLS' HOUSES AND MINIATURES

Architecture for Dolls' Houses — *Joyce Percival*
Beginners' Guide to the Dolls' House Hobby — *Jean Nisbett*
The Complete Dolls' House Book — *Jean Nisbett*
The Dolls' House 1/24 Scale: A Complete Introduction — *Jean Nisbett*
Dolls' House Accessories, Fixtures and Fittings — *Andrea Barham*
Dolls' House Bathrooms: Lots of Little Loos — *Patricia King*
Dolls' House Fireplaces and Stoves — *Patricia King*
Easy to Make Dolls' House Accessories — *Andrea Barham*
Heraldic Miniature Knights — *Peter Greenhill*
Make Your Own Dolls' House Furniture — *Maurice Harper*
Making Dolls' House Furniture — *Patricia King*
Making Georgian Dolls' Houses — *Derek Rowbottom*
Making Miniature Gardens — *Freida Gray*
Making Miniature Oriental Rugs & Carpets — *Meik & Ian McNaughton*
Making Period Dolls' House Accessories — *Andrea Barham*
Making Period Dolls' House Furniture — *Derek & Sheila Rowbottom*
Making Tudor Dolls' Houses — *Derek Rowbottom*
Making Unusual Miniatures — *Graham Spalding*
Making Victorian Dolls' House Furniture — *Patricia King*
Miniature Bobbin Lace — *Roz Snowden*
Miniature Embroidery for the Victorian Dolls' House — *Pamela Warner*
Miniature Embroidery for the Georgian Dolls' House — *Pamela Warner*
Miniature Needlepoint Carpets — *Janet Granger*
The Secrets of the Dolls' House Makers — *Jean Nisbett*

CRAFTS

American Patchwork Designs in Needlepoint — *Melanie Tacon*
A Beginners' Guide to Rubber Stamping — *Brenda Hunt*
Celtic Cross Stitch Designs — *Carol Phillipson*
Celtic Knotwork Designs — *Sheila Sturrock*
Celtic Knotwork Handbook — *Sheila Sturrock*
Collage from Seeds, Leaves and Flowers — *Joan Carver*
Complete Pyrography — *Stephen Poole*
Contemporary Smocking — *Dorothea Hall*
Creating Knitwear Designs — *Pat Ashforth & Steve Plummer*
Creative Doughcraft — *Patricia Hughes*
Creative Embroidery Techniques
    Using Colour Through Gold — *Daphne J. Ashby & Jackie Woolsey*
The Creative Quilter: Techniques and Projects — *Pauline Brown*
Cross Stitch Kitchen Projects — *Janet Granger*
Cross Stitch on Colour — *Sheena Rogers*
Decorative Beaded Purses — *Enid Taylor*
Designing and Making Cards — *Glennis Gilruth*
Embroidery Tips & Hints — *Harold Hayes*
Glass Painting — *Emma Sedman*
An Introduction to Crewel Embroidery — *Mave Glenny*
Making and Using Working Drawings for Realistic Model Animals — *Basil F. Fordham*
Making Character Bears — *Valerie Tyler*
Making Greetings Cards for Beginners — *Pat Sutherland*
Making Hand-Sewn Boxes: Techniques and Projects — *Jackie Woolsey*
Making Knitwear Fit — *Pat Ashforth & Steve Plummer*
Natural Ideas for Christmas: Fantastic Decorations to Make — *Josie Cameron-Ashcroft and Carol Cox*
Needlepoint: A Foundation Course — *Sandra Hardy*
Pyrography Designs — *Norma Gregory*
Pyrography Handbook (Practical Crafts) — *Stephen Poole*
Ribbons and Roses — *Lee Lockheed*
Rubber Stamping with Other Crafts — *Lynne Garner*
Sponge Painting — *Ann Rooney*
Tassel Making for Beginners — *Enid Taylor*
Tatting Collage — *Lindsay Rogers*
Temari: A Traditional Japanese Embroidery Technique — *Margaret Ludlow*
Theatre Models in Paper and Card — *Robert Burgess*
Wool Embroidery and Design — *Lee Lockheed*

HOME & GARDEN

Bird Boxes and Feeders for the Garden — *Dave Mackenzie*
The Birdwatcher's Garden — *Hazel and Pamela Johnson*
Home Ownership: Buying and Maintaining — *Nicholas Snelling*
The Living Tropical Greenhouse: Creating a Haven for Butterflies — *John and Maureen Tampion*
Security for the Householder: Fitting Locks and Other Devices — *E. Phillips*

VIDEOS

Drop-in and Pinstuffed Seats	*David James*
Stuffover Upholstery	*David James*
Elliptical Turning	*David Springett*
Woodturning Wizardry	*David Springett*
Turning Between Centres: The Basics	*Dennis White*
Turning Bowls	*Dennis White*
Boxes, Goblets and Screw Threads	*Dennis White*
Novelties and Projects	*Dennis White*
Classic Profiles	*Dennis White*

Twists and Advanced Turning	*Dennis White*
Sharpening the Professional Way	*Jim Kingshott*
Sharpening Turning & Carving Tools	*Jim Kingshott*
Bowl Turning	*John Jordan*
Hollow Turning	*John Jordan*
Woodturning: A Foundation Course	*Keith Rowley*
Carving a Figure: The Female Form	*Ray Gonzalez*
The Router: A Beginner's Guide	*Alan Goodsell*
The Scroll Saw: A Beginner's Guide	*John Burke*

MAGAZINES

WOODTURNING ◆ WOODCARVING ◆ FURNITURE & CABINETMAKING
THE DOLLS' HOUSE MAGAZINE ◆ CREATIVE CRAFTS FOR THE HOME
THE ROUTER ◆ THE SCROLLSAW ◆ BUSINESSMATTERS
WATER GARDENING

The above represents a full list of all titles currently published or scheduled to be published.
All are available direct from the Publishers or through bookshops, newsagents and specialist retailers.
To place an order, or to obtain a complete catalogue, contact:

GMC Publications,
Castle Place, 166 High Street, Lewes, East Sussex BN7 1XU, United Kingdom
Tel: 01273 488005 Fax: 01273 478606

Orders by credit card are accepted